101

MINDFUL

WAYS BUILD
TO
RESILIENCE

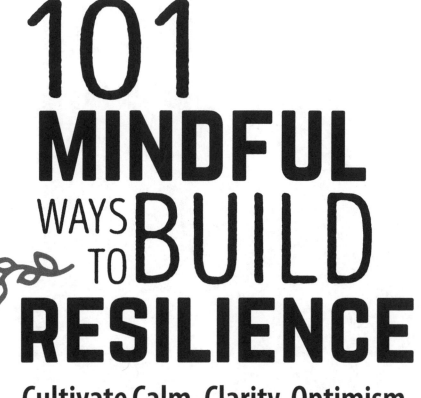

Cultivate Calm, Clarity, Optimism & Happiness Each Day

Donald Altman, MA, LPC

Bestselling author of
The Mindfulness Toolbox and *One-Minute Mindfulness*

"Delightful. Wise. Practical. Altman immediately brings the reader into a mindful moment. He makes the cultivation of calm, clarity, optimism and happiness not only doable but inviting—and it's one minute at a time. Nurture resilience and joy not by blocking whatever may be difficult, but through acknowledgment, acceptance and appreciation. This book helps us remember that where we place our attention makes a difference. It empowers us to build resilience every day."

— **Elana Rosenbaum, MS, MSW, BCD,** pioneer teacher of mindfulness-based stress reduction, psychotherapist and speaker, author of *Being Well (even when you're sick): Mindfulness Practices* and *Here for Now: Living Well with Cancer Through Mindfulness.*

"Donald Altman's *101 Mindful Ways to Build Resilience* is the essential resilience toolkit for business leaders or anyone wanting bold and practical methods for turning obstacles into success. This book provides real-world advice about how to turn self-doubt and negative thinking into affirmation of one's own abilities. It is filled with innovative and engaging mindfulness methods for enhancing people skills and building resiliency. Whether reinvigorating your career or striving for excellence, this must-read book will enhance your attitude and life with greater clarity, confidence, and optimism! I highly recommend it!"

— **John Baldoni,** author of bestselling *MOXIE: The Secret to Bold and Gutsy Leadership* and *Lead with Purpose.*

"Each minute-long chapter will help you create that special mindful space to enrich not only the rest of your day, but the rest of your life."

— **Jean L. Kristeller, PhD,** author of *The Joy of Half a Cookie: Using Mindfulness to Lose Weight* and *End the Struggle with Food*

Copyright © 2016 by Donald Altman

Published by:
PESI Publishing and Media
PESI, Inc.
3839 White Ave
Eau Claire, WI 54703

Printed in the United States of America

Cover & Page Design: Matt Pabich
Edited by: Karsyn Morse, Hillary Jenness
  & Marietta Whittlesey

ISBN: 9781559570466

The information in this book is meant only for
educational purposes, and not as a substitute for
mental health professional care or medical advice.
No implied or expressed guarantee regarding the
effects of these recommendations or practices can be
given, and no liability assumed.

 PESI
Publishing
& Media
www.pesipublishing.com

Donald Altman, MA, LPC,

is a psychotherapist, former Buddhist monk, and award-winning author. A past Vice-President of The Center for Mindful Eating, he serves on the TCME advisory board. Donald is currently an adjunct professor in the Interpersonal Neurobiology program at Portland State University, and has also taught at Lewis and Clark College Graduate School of Education and Counseling.

Donald conducts mindful living and mindful eating workshops and retreats internationally and has trained thousands of mental health therapists and healthcare workers on how to use mindfulness as a tool for managing depression, anxiety, pain, and stress. He is known as America's Mindfulness Coach for the way he integrates timeless mindfulness tools, neuroscience, and spiritual values into modern life. Donald trained with the venerable U Silananda, author of *The Four Foundations of Mindfulness,* at a Buddhist monastery located near the San Bernardino Mountains in Southern California. He is a member of the Burma Buddhist Monastery Association.

A prolific writer whose career spans more than 30 years, Donald's *The Mindfulness Toolbox* won two gold Benjamin Franklin awards as the best book in the mind-body-spirit and psychology categories in 2015. *The Mindfulness Code* was selected as "one of the best spiritual books of 2010." Donald has also written for an Emmy Award winning children's television program, and has had numerous articles appear in print. An avid motorcyclist, Donald enjoys riding along the Oregon coast. He lives in Portland, Oregon.

For information about Donald Altman's books, guided meditation CDs, workshops, speaking, and consulting services, visit www.MindfulPractices.com

content

acknowledgement

My deepest gratitude extends to all those individuals who have dedicated themselves to sharing teachings of peace and mindfulness with others. I thank my late teacher, the Venerable U Silananda, who was a dedicated mindfulness guide for many years; Ashin Thitzana, a spiritual friend and monk brother who lives and inspires others through his teachings of the dharma; U Thondara and the monks and community of the Burma Buddhist Monastery; Maria Brignola, a dance movement therapist and teacher, for helping me recognize the need for a book blending mindfulness and resilience, as well as for her on target guidance and feedback along the way; Randy Fitzgerald, a friend and talented writer whose insights and intuitions always prompted new creative leaps; Friends Greg Crosby, Jeff Horacek and others who acted as sounding boards and provided useful feedback.

I want to thank Linda Jackson, Publisher, for always being supportive and collaborative every step of the way—a writer's dream—even brainstorming initial concepts for the book as we walked through Mall of America in Bloomington, Minnesota; The PESI Publishing & Media family, including Mike Olson, Karsyn Morse, Claire Zelasko, Emily Bauer, Marnie Sullivan, Anna Rustick, Matt Pabich, and others too numerous to mention, who have worked tirelessly to help my books and workshops reach healthcare professionals and others.

This book would not have been possible without so many the friends, colleagues, teachers, clients, acquaintances, students, etc. — who have served daily as my gifted and courageous co-explorers of resilience. I am particularly indebted to my father Norman, and mother Barbara, who always had an encouraging word and continues to support my creative work.

Especially, I wish to thank Maria Brignola for helping me open and heal my heart, and for inviting me on a journey to the heart through her kind and loving support of this project. Maria, you are my *Bak'u del cuore*.

introduction

How important is a minute? How many minutes did you really pay attention to today, even before reading this? Did the little in-between moments slip by unnoticed because you were caught in distraction? Or, were your minutes populated by thoughts of worrisome stories or fears? Did you ever stop to think how a single minute, *this very next minute,* holds the potential to change the direction of your thoughts, your life? How this next 60 seconds can act as a storehouse of resilience to help you bounce back from daily challenges, difficulties, and hardships?

No one is immune from life's many obstacles. To live with a human body and a human mind means having to confront grief, loss, disappointment, frustration, and even illusion. Fortunately, that is only part of the story. While you cannot control the cards you are dealt your in life, you can decide how to best play your hand—in this upcoming minute. It is this truth that is fortifying and encouraging.

How you respond to life's stumbling blocks and hurdles right here, right now, in the next 60 seconds, can make all the difference.

To explore if there might be a better way, take a moment to ask yourself the following:

Has my mental treadmill of worries or rumination ever really solved anything for me?

Have I felt true contentment, clarity, happiness, and optimism when I'm not present, but stuck in thoughts about the past or future?

There is a more life-enhancing way. It is an approach that reduces needless suffering by harnessing the power of mindfulness, attention, and the daily resilience practices in this book. That is why *101 Mindful Ways to Build Resilience* is based upon the following idea—

Where and how you use your awareness in this next minute determines the very quality of your life—your ability to live joyfully, to accept the present conditions of the precious life you have, and to bounce back from life's most challenging obstacles.

In one minute you can utilize the astounding power of your attention to sharpen your focus in new ways that bring contentment, clarity, happiness, and optimism— in other words, the core foundations of resilience. The mindfulness experiences in this book tap into the body, the mind, and relationships with others as we manifest our deepest values in this next minute. If you question whether this is possible, that's not surprising! After all, most of us are taught that change is difficult and takes a long time. If you've ever tried to stay on a diet, you may believe change is nearly impossible. In fact, most diets fail because they ask you to follow a rigid set of rules.

I only ask one thing—that you enter this moment with curiosity and openness. For it is in this moment that you can choose a new direction that resonates with you, rather than strictly follow a joyless and empty set of rules or obligations about how things are supposed to be.

Before jumping in, look over this list, and as you do, use your imagination to picture how it would feel for you to experience the following. Visualize, too, how each of these choices could be possible—even for a single minute.

> *This next precious breath.*
>
> *The sights and sounds of someone you care about.*
>
> *Ordinary appreciation for what comes to your door right now*
> *—both the pleasant and the unpleasant.*
>
> *Letting go of unreasonable life expectations and rigid rules.*
>
> *Softening your heart to even the unwanted things in your life.*
>
> *Being a compassionate presence for others.*
>
> *Opening the heart of giving.*
>
> *Tapping the wisdom of this minute.*
>
> *Cultivating a new and beautiful garden of thought in this minute.*

The positive, supportive, and life-changing possibilities inherent in this next minute are infinite. These integrate your whole being—body, mind, and spirit—by inviting the entire experience that life has to offer. My hope is that these 101 simple practices will act as a springboard for you to shape a fruitful and fulfilling life as you rewire your brain for resiliency. Best of all, you can undertake this journey one minute at a time. How marvelous!

calm

Resilience would be nearly impossible if you were constantly upset, irritated, irrational, and beset by a host of negative feelings. Calm is the magic elixir that brings you to a place of balance, harmony, and peace. It is from this emotionally centered point of view that you are more prepared and capable of making compassionate, caring, and sensible choices for yourself and others.

reboot your brain with this precious breath 1

Anytime that you are emotionally triggered, reactive, or defensive, the part of your brain that does the thinking, judging, analyzing, and decision-making actually goes offline—it's like losing your Internet connection or having your computer's hard drive fail. Fortunately, you don't need to wait for a computer tech. You only need to take a long, slow breath that calms and relaxes the body and reboots your thinking brain.

HOW

1. Find a quiet place where you can sit undisturbed. Settle into your chair. Feel your feet on the floor and your body contacting the chair.

2. Assume an erect and dignified, but relaxed posture as you bring awareness to your breath. Get curious about each in-breath and out-breath, realizing that no two breaths are alike.

3. Visualize your belly or abdominal area like a balloon. Inhaling, picture the balloon expanding as it fills up. If you've been holding the stomach in, give yourself permission to let the muscles relax so it can soften and move.

4. Exhale slowly, letting the breath go out for a count of three or four. You don't have to count it, but just feel the slow release of air. If the stomach area is not moving, move your arms behind your back and clasp your hands together. This position opens the rib cage to make belly breathing easier.

WHEN

Practice anytime you feel upset, triggered by a craving, or reactive. If possible, separate physically from what is causing you to be reactive. After calming down, use your thinking brain to respond differently. Continue to breathe as often as needed—one minute at a time.

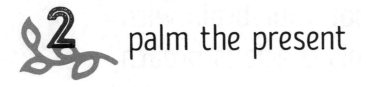# palm the present

In his essay *Walking,* Henry David Thoreau wrote that while he was making his way around Walden Pond, "…The thought of some work will run in my head, and I am not where my body is….What business have I in the woods if I am thinking of something out of the woods?" And he didn't have a cell phone to distract him. That's why, when we're lost in thought, a good way to find ourselves is to simply "return to our senses" via the body.

HOW

1. Begin sitting or standing. After settling in, raise your hands in front of the your chest, with hands about a foot apart.

2. Slowly bring your hands together, pausing the moment you sense any heat, warmth, energy, or pressure.

3. Continue to bring the hands together until the fingertips lightly touch.

4. Bring the hands closer until the palms touch. Notice how the fingers straighten and how the hands make contact.

5. Raise your elbows up and press your palms together fairly hard for the count of five (less if you feel pain).

6. Lower the elbows and relax the shoulders to let go of the tension. Open your hands as you let the arms come down to rest onto your legs.

7. Imagine breathing into the body where any tension remains. Exhale the tension out with the breath—picturing it draining out down the legs and out the bottom of your feet and back into the Earth for recycling.

WHEN

Use this to get centered anytime you feel overwhelmed, stressed, distracted, or lost in negative thinking.

this soothing moment

Negativity and anxiety and reactivity are like filters that block out the light. Let's remove these shades by noticing one soothing thing in the next minute. This practice shifts awareness and changes how your brain pays attention because it takes you off autopilot and gently guides you to enter this moment in a safe and soothing way. Do this portable exercise anywhere, sitting or standing, at home or at work, while walking or driving your car, or in your backyard.

✤ HOW ✤

1. Broaden your gaze and sensitivity. Imagine that you could be aware of everything all around you using your senses.

2. For the next minute, tune in to all the smallest details of colors, sounds, shapes, textures, temperature, people, and natural or man-made objects in your surroundings.

3. Find one soothing thing. This might be a favorite color, the sense of safety you feel, the comfortable ambient temperature, or even a memory that comes from noticing something that is soothing to you. If you find more than one thing and that's okay, too.

4. Allow yourself to savor this soothing thing in great detail for another minute.

5. Take a mental snapshot or use your phone to take an actual photo that you can save in a 'soothing moments' file.

✤ WHEN ✤

Notice one soothing thing each time you pass through a doorway and enter a new space. Use this practice when you are dwelling on negative thoughts. Keep a one-minute soothing moments file or journal, so you can review these moments and share them with others.

4 calibrate and tame your emotions

Have your emotions ever gotten the best of you? It happens. Yes, we need our emotions—but when reactive emotions are allowed to run the show, we can be left feeling drained, as well as behave in ways that we may later regret. This practice helps you *name the emotion in order to tame the emotion*.

ᢟ HOW ᢞ

1. Physically separate yourself, if necessary, from the stress or situation that is producing your high level of emotional reactivity. Go to a neutral corner—meaning find a place of silence where you can be alone for a minute or so.

2. Take three calming breaths.

3. Name the primary emotion that you are feeling. The process of naming the emotion—anger, frustration, sadness, etc.—forces you to use the thinking brain.

4. Name other emotions that are also present, such as hurt, loneliness, or disappointment, and so on. Multiple emotions are often present, so take your time and name them all.

5. Where in the body do you sense the emotion(s)? The gut, the heart area, the shoulders, etc.?

6. Now, consider how you can respond differently in the future to the situation or event that triggered your emotion. By naming the emotion, you paused to observe and constructively distance from it—instead of simply reacting. Congratulations on deepening your understanding and changing your relationship to the emotion.

ᢟ WHEN ᢞ

Use this practice anytime you feel overwhelmed, stressed out, or reactive. Name the emotion when you first begin to sense it. This will help you calibrate and tame emotions—even those strongly ingrained ones—more quickly and effectively.

tone up your vagus nerve 5

Did you know that you have a built-in nerve whose purpose it is to regulate and relax you? The vagus nerve is the longest cranial nerve. This vital nerve pathway traverses the inside of the spine as it links up the brain with the heart and the gut. Here's a simple, ancient practice for observing the breath that activates the vagus nerve in order to relax the body and brain as it buffers you from stress. This technique is taught to Navy SEALs to help them focus and stay calm during challenging missions.

✺ HOW ✺

1. Bring the palms of your hands together in front of your chest

2. Spend a few moments noticing the warmth between your palms to get centered.

3. Inhale and fill your belly with air as you simultaneously move both arms outwards—as if you were opening up an accordion.

4. When your arms are spread fully outwards, hold the breath for the count of two.

5. Exhale slowly while counting to four and moving your arms inward until your palms come back together. Make sure you let out all the air.

6. Repeat this breathing practice 3-5 times at a sitting, standing, or lying down.

✺ WHEN ✺

Consider using this simple, yet powerful, calming practice anytime you feel stressed or overwhelmed. It is also an excellent way to counter anxiety—such as prior to a stressful business meeting, appointment, exam, or driving on a congested freeway (use it before driving). It's also ideal for calming down *after* a stressful experience.

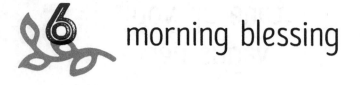

morning blessing

Morning is a special time, a sacred time in the sense that it harkens our return to the world of daily activity. But waking up in the morning is more than just being conscious and cognitively awake. Awakening is a metaphor for how you wake up to appreciating each new day in a meaningful, playful, creative, and thoughtful way.

❧ HOW ❧

1. Create a morning blessing. A special morning blessing of thanks and gratitude can be stated or written in the morning, or created in advance. This blessing will help you shift into a place of ease and grace.

2. For your blessing, focus on a single and simple gratitude—such as appreciating your body, the warm bed that you slept on, the fresh water that brings you life and health, and the relationships that bring joy.

3. Make a point of appreciating one new thing each morning.

4. No gratitude is too small or simple.

5. Have your morning blessing at your bedside or someplace you will remember it. You can even tape it to the bathroom mirror.

6. At some point in the morning, repeat your blessing and notice how it changes your day and makes you feel.

❧ WHEN ❧

Save your morning blessings so you can look back over them. Mentally repeat your blessing throughout the morning. You may even expand your awareness of gratitude. In this way, you open up to the good and decent things in your life, as well as increase your ability to stay connected to thankfulness.

daily intention setting

Each day most of us act upon hundreds of unconscious intentions, often mindlessly and without a second thought. In contrast, a consciously thought out intention aligns you with your deepest values. It helps you *show up* in a way that makes even your smallest actions count. A guiding intention invites a sense of order and calm into your day—and life.

ৡ HOW ৡ

1. Start with a daily intention that is small and simple. This could be your intention to treat others with respect and kindness, to be more compassionate, honest, or more peaceful and less reactive when encountering triggering events or persons during your day.

2. State your intentions in the positive, not the negative. A daily intention can focus on almost anything, from a significant relationship to your role at the workplace. An example is, "May I act with respect and integrity in the workplace, and my intention is to meet my deadlines and perform to my best ability with a positive attitude."

3. Write down your daily intention and carry it with you. Take as much time as you need to reflect upon your deeper intentions. Each need only be a sentence or two long.

4. Look at your intention throughout the day so it informs how you speak and act.

ৡ WHEN ৡ

Find a quiet place to state your daily intention. Take a minute or two to let it seep into your being. Set the same intention over the period of a week to allow it to take hold. And of course, feel free to rewrite any intention as needed.

 # evening blessing

While a morning blessing greets the day, an evening blessing brings you a sense of closure. This is an important opportunity to reflect on the day. Your evening blessing is like the gift that you wrap up and give yourself each night as you leave the world of action and enter the world of rest and repose.

❧ HOW ❧

1. Think back over your day. Recall one unexpected positive event or response from another for which you are thankful.

2. There are no unimportant moments; even a smile from a stranger is a kindness for which you could be grateful. Let yourself remember all those little moments that you savored and appreciated. How wonderful!

3. Notice all that is present in your life—even those things you normally take for granted. State your gratitude for that which this day has provided.

4. End your blessing by sending your wish for rest, peace, love, and wellness to others. Include family and friends, and even those people you know only as acquaintances. If you want, expand your blessing to include all beings.

❧ WHEN ❧

Think of your evening blessing as a ritual that soothes and prepares you for sleep and rejuvenation. Because rituals bring a sense of order and calm into our lives, repeat your blessing at the same time each night in a way that lets you be fully present. This might mean lighting a candle, lowering the lights, taking a long breath, or placing your palms over your heart center. Consider sharing this special moment of daily closure with another.

sleep ritual

One of the best ways to repair and renew the body and brain after a long day is to get a good night's sleep. For example, daytime learning gets consolidated into long-term memory while sleeping. It is while sleeping that toxic wastes are removed from the brain—a recently discovered process important for brain health. A sleep ritual can help you achieve a peaceful slumber.

ᔊ HOW ᔊ

1. Set a time for sleep. Go to bed at the same time each night—even during weekends—because you are training your body's sleep clock.

2. Prepare for sleep *an hour before* your bedtime. Design your ritual to create a soothing and calming entry to sleep. Change into comfortable clothes, listen to soft music, savor a cup of non-caffeinated tea, light a candle, read something enjoyable, or take a calming hot bath.

3. Power off the TV, computer, and tablets. That's because the electroluminescent light from these devices can delay production of the hormone melatonin—which makes you feel drowsy and sets the body's sleep clock—by up to an hour or more.

4. Remove or reduce sources of light from your bedroom.

5. Mentally let go of any to-do list or things you may be thinking about. It may help to write these down or visualize putting them into a lock-box where they will be kept safe until morning.

ᔊ WHEN ᔊ

The key to making a sleep ritual effective is consistency and repetition. If you've had trouble sleeping, give yourself time to let this work. Even if it takes a month or longer, your body will eventually get the message.

10 be-this grounding and centering

The word 'centering' means getting very balanced, grounded, and present in the here and now. Think of how a tree is literally anchored to the ground. "BE-THIS" is an acronym that stands for six powerful grounding and centering skills that get you rooted and secure (Breath, Emotion, Touch, Hearing, Intentional Stretching, Sight/Smell). This process helps you feel safer and calmer because it puts you in touch with your senses and brings the wandering mind back from those unsupervised trips to Anxiety Land and Dwellsville.

HOW

1. **B**reathe. Take two or three soothing diaphragmatic breaths.

2. **E**motion. Tune in to your emotional state. Name or label your emotions like you learned in Chapter 4, *Calibrate and Tame Your Emotions*.

3. **T**ouch. Briskly rub your palms together for a few seconds. Next, place your hands over your eyes, then one hand over each temple, then one on your forehead and the other over the back of your head. Feel the soothing energy from your hands.

4. **H**ear. Tune into the sounds of your environment. Notice as many different and subtle sounds as you can.

5. **I**ntentional Stretching. Lift your shoulders up and down or move your head from side to side in a relaxing circular motion.

6. **S**ight/Smell. Finally, simply look around and notice *in detail* as many different scents, shapes, sizes, and colors as you can—noticing these with child-like wonder.

WHEN

Practice BE-THIS at home so that when you need it you won't have to think about it. It will just come naturally. Use it whenever you feel scattered, stressed, overwhelmed or even before an anxiety-provoking situation.

snack with calm abiding

Did you ever just gulp down a snack without even tasting it? By slowing down and really tasting the snack, you reverse the pattern of stress eating and feel more in control as you nourish yourself. This is an act of self-care. Instead of making food a pleasure race, you make it a place to find grace.

✺ HOW ✺

Find a quiet place to eat, even if it's a work cubicle. Turn off distractions.

1. Before eating (or ordering) ask, "What am I hungry for? What flavors and textures would satisfy this hunger? How much food would satisfy this hunger?"

2. Take a calming breath and appreciate your food. Before eating, appreciate the natural energy and human effort contained in this food.

3. Take the first bite focusing on selections. Select the size of the bite, where in the mouth to chew, how fast you want to chew, and when to swallow.

4. Take the second bite focusing on taste. Where in the mouth and tongue do you vividly notice the flavor? How does this change from bite to bite?

5. Take the third bite focusing on observation. Observe your munching and how food turns from solid to liquid. See how long the flavor of each bite lasts, the movement of the jaw, and even your thoughts.

6. For the fourth bite, pause. Put down the utensil and take a breath.

✺ WHEN ✺

Use this for one snack a day to start. You might be surprised how this slows you down and lets you know the difference between being fulfilled with food as opposed to filling up.

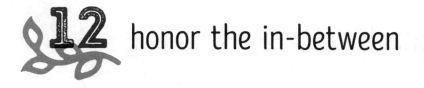# 12 honor the in-between

Getting to any destination is highly overrated. Whether it's an appointment, getting to work, finishing that paper or project, getting the grade, etc., arriving at the destination is like the punctuation point, or period, marking the end of the sentence. Yes, you've reached the goal—but that is a sliver of your experience. The in-between time is like the entire descriptive sentence. It gives context and color to the destination and tells the complete story of how you arrived and lived.

❧ HOW ❧

1. Begin by identifying your in-between time, such as anytime you are waiting to reach a goal: Walking to get the mail; shopping in a store before checking out; driving on the freeway going to and from work; when the commercial plays on the TV or radio.

2. How do you feel when you're in-between? Create a log of your in-between time moods. Is there boredom, frustration, impatience, or anger?

3. Honor your in-between time by soothing yourself or connecting with others.

4. Smell the roses along the way, so to speak, by noticing pleasant things in your in-between travels—even if you're moving along the hallway in your home.

5. Be curious and flexible as you move toward your destination. If you find something unusual along the way, give yourself permission to honor and experience it.

❧ WHEN ❧

Honor the in-between by letting it be part of the destination. In this way, each step, each in-between moment counts. By savoring your in-between, you will feel more alive and be more present.

sun breathing 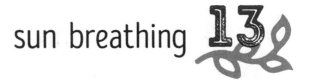 13

Has your mind wandered today? Scientists have found that on average, our minds wander almost fifty percent of the time. Interestingly, they found that when people were very present and not mind-wandering—such as when exercising or engaged in conversation—they rated themselves as most happy and content. In *One-Minute Mindfulness*, I wrote, "Your breath is your intimate kiss with this moment." Contentment is only a sun breath away.

✤ HOW ✤

1. Find a place to sit or stand—in the sunlight if possible. But it doesn't have to be sunny outside because you can always visualize yourself beneath a bright, warm sun.

2. Imagine that as you inhale, you can absorb the warm light of the sun into your body.

3. Inhale as you slowly raise your arms out to the sides and over your head like the sun rising in the morning sky. As you inhale and feel your abdomen expand, visualize the energy of the sun filling up all your cells. Hold this breath for 2-3 seconds.

4. Exhale slowly as you gently lower your arms.

5. When your arms are outstretched at your sides—and with both palms facing up to the sky—pause for another three sun-breaths.

6. With each breath, imagine that your palms are like solar panels soaking up the warm and life-producing energy of the sun. With each sun breath, let your palms grow warm and soft. Feel them directing the energy of contentment and calm to wherever you need it in your body.

✤ WHEN ✤

Use sun breathing anytime your mind wanders in dis-contentment, is stuck in a mental rut, or whenever you need a solar powered lift.

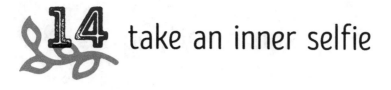# 14 take an inner selfie

Perhaps more important than the messages you "post" on social networks are the inner "mental snapshots" that are posted by your mind-body network—all of which can be thought of as *taking an inner selfie.* How your *inner selfie* looks can determine whether you feel anxious, depressed, happy, or secure. Before changing an *inner selfie,* you first need to recognize it.

❧ HOW ❧

1. Picture yourself as an impartial observer who has a camera that can distance from your mind and take *inner selfies* at any time during the day.

2. Take an *inner selfie* right now. What did you discover about the subject of your quick inner snapshot? What are you thinking and feeling?

3. Cultivate an attitude of openness, self-kindness, and curiosity toward each *selfie* snapshot, whether it shows dissatisfaction, anxiety, sadness, or even criticism about your taking a selfie.

4. Accept your existing *selfie,* remembering with inner hospitality that it is only a thought—and it doesn't define you.

5. Notice if there's a particular theme to your *selfies.* Do these mental "posts" remind you of anyone? If you could, how would you like to change your *selfies?*

6. Make a new *selfie* post right now—one that helps you feel secure, safe, and centered. You can post a new mental *inner selfie* simply by finding a new perspective.

❧ WHEN ❧

Get in the habit of taking *inner selfies* throughout the day. This skill lets you be more accepting and at peace with your mind. Congratulations on being an excellent *inner selfie* observer. By taking *inner selfies* you are no longer mindlessly reacting to the thoughts, moods, and cravings that you may encounter.

breathing out stress 15 visualization

Scientists now know that stress gets under the skin and can change hundreds of biological processes related to hormone production, the immune system, and aging. Wouldn't it be nice if there were an easy way to counter stress? Fortunately, there is a simple visualization for draining out negative emotion, stress, and tension from the body.

❧ HOW ☙

1. Find a safe and quiet place where you can spend a minute or two. You can sit, stand or lie down for this practice.

2. Starting from the feet, slowly scan upwards from the bottom of your feet as you tune in to the body. Sense for any stress, tightness, tension, blockage, or negative emotions. This might be in the muscles or it could be an emotional feeling of heaviness in the gut, heart, or other areas.

3. Take an in-breath, visualize the breath entering your body as a healing white or golden light. See the light enter through the nose, mouth, or the crown of the head.

4. Let the light go directly to wherever you are feeling stress, tension or negative emotion. Picture the light fill up all the cells in the afflicted part of the body.

5. Exhale slowly. Visualize your breath carrying all the tension or negativity down the body, down the legs, and out the bottom of the feet—where it deposits all that negative energy into the Earth for recycling. Take as many balancing breaths as needed.

❧ WHEN ☙

This is a portable practice that you can do almost anywhere and anytime you feel tense or emotionally unbalanced.

16 change your body, change your mind

Did you know that your posture and facial expressions can change how you think? Scientists used Botox to freeze the frowning muscles in the faces of subjects and discovered that those individuals had a difficult time conceptualizing thoughts around anger and sadness. That's because they couldn't make the facial expression that went with the thought. Follow these steps to shift your body in order to positively alter your mood and mind.

❧ HOW ☙

1. Throughout the day, notice your posture—particularly when you feel negative, stressed, or anxious. Does your body tighten up? Where? Do you tend to look up, down, or away from others?

2. Assume a more relaxed and open posture. Make sure your arms, hands and jaw are relaxed and not clenched or tight. Avoid crossing your arms over your chest, which makes it harder to take a calming breath. Do you notice a difference?

3. Experiment with smiling. Smile for the next thirty seconds and see how this changes how you feel and maybe even think.

4. Try the following different body movements and expressions: A confident posture and facial expression. A compassionate one. A loving one.

5. Look at the postures and expressions of those you admire. When they speak or act, is their body in alignment with their mood? Practice by experimenting with the postures and expressions of those you want to emulate.

❧ WHEN ☙

This is an intriguing and powerful way of altering fixed mindsets. Use it anytime you feel defensive, stuck in anger, or want to change your mood on the spot.

anchored breathing

Distractions often draw us away from staying with awareness of the breath. This practice will draw upon the earlier breath practices (see: Practices 1 and 5) as it strengthens your ability to remain present with the breath. Research shows that focusing on the breath both reduces mind wandering and lessens negative thinking.

HOW

1. Find a quiet place to sit where you won't be interrupted.

2. As you breathe, locate the place(s) in the body where you most vividly notice the in-breath and out-breath. For example, the physical sensation of breath might be most vivid in the nasal passage, the back of the throat, the expansion of the lungs, or the movement of the shoulders or stomach. There is no right or wrong place to notice your breath.

3. This vivid physical contact point acts as an anchor, a place you can return time and again when you get distracted.

4. This anchor point might be the same for the in-breath and out-breath, or you might notice different anchor points. By finding your personal anchor point you are taking ownership of your own breath. Each time you breathe you might find the anchor point has changed, and that's okay.

5. Now that you've pinpointed where you feel the breath in your body, breathe for one minute while focusing on the anchor point. If your mind wanders, that's okay. Gently bring attention back to your anchor point.

WHEN

Practice anchored breath three minutes a day (or more) to calm, de-stress, and stabilize your mind as you teach it to pay attention to what's happening now.

 uni-walking

Technology may be changing how we move and walk. It's not unheard of for people using cell phones to bump into lamp posts or to step off curbs. Uni-walking means walking just to walk, with full awareness and presence. When mind and body are in the same place, an accident is less likely to happen. Best of all, you'll experience the joy of taking this next step. Uni-walking can be experienced as this process:

✖ HOW ✖

1. Set the *intention* to take a step. This might seem redundant or silly, but intention focuses you into consciously doing what it is that you are doing.

2. Follow-up with the *action* of taking this next step.

3. Closely *observe* what it is like to take that step as your foot lifts off the floor, your knee pivots and moves the foot forward, your foot and leg lower and the heel touches the ground, and how your weight pivots from one side of the body to the other. (Who knew so much was going on?)

4. You can also set intentions for turning your body in a new direction.

5. Move at whatever pace works best, whether slow, normal, or brisk, so long as your balance is not compromised.

6. Optionally, set one overall intention to just "walk" as you place awareness on all the movements of uni-walking.

✖ WHEN ✖

Shift into uni-walking anytime you feel the need to calm and rest the weary mind, get a little space from it all, or when feeling anxiety during a transition from one place to another.

stoplight meditation

Have you ever felt like stoplights conspire to make you late by turning red just as you approach the intersection? Believe it or not, you can transform red light frustration into something that brings you peace and serenity. Though this might seem impossible, the stoplight meditation can, ironically, turn a stoplight into a "move forward with ease" signal. Red lights give you about a minute's worth of meditation time to reset how you are feeling.

❧ HOW ☙

1. When the car comes to a stop, turn off the radio and other distractions. Place your hands on the lower portion of the steering wheel, a position which makes it easier to bring the breath into the belly.

2. Begin by noticing the breath. Deepen and slow down your breath.

3. Expand awareness to how you are sitting in the seat. Feel your back on the seatback and your bottom on the seat cushion.

4. Sense how your palms and fingers wrap around the steering wheel. Notice the texture and temperature of the surface of the steering wheel.

5. Listen for all the sounds in and out of the car. Can you hear the engine? Your own breath?

6. Appreciate one thing that is pleasant inside or out of the car—a color, shape, sound, or natural object.

7. When the light turns green, send a blessing of safe travels to yourself and fellow drivers around you.

❧ WHEN ☙

Use this whenever you get frustrated while driving, as well as for releasing tension on the way home after a stressful workday.

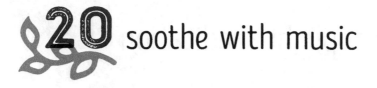# 20 soothe with music

Music does much more than just stimulate the auditory nerve. The vibrations of music get translated deep into the brain's emotional core and result in a dance of hormones and neurotransmitters. This hormonal dance dramatically shifts your mood and can affect numerous bodily systems, including respiration, blood pressure, and even the immune system. The right music can prime you for feelings of deep calm, serenity, and joy.

❧ HOW ❧

1. Identify the kind of music that makes you feel calm, upbeat, relaxed, joyful, or peaceful. Music is very personal, and there's a wide variety of music you can use—from classical to rock. For a serene and meditative state, consider spiritual songs such as *Amazing Grace, Somewhere Over the Rainbow,* and *Ave Maria.*

2. For one minute or longer, play your favorite soothing music. If you don't have the music with you, simply sing the lyrics out loud or "in your head."

3. After a minute of hearing the music, make a note of how you feel. Become aware of body sensations, as well as slight shifts in mood or thought patterns. Does your breath become slower, fuller? Do your muscles feel relaxed? Are you reminded of any places or images that soothe you?

4. Keep a log of music to compare various tunes and explore the different feelings they elicit.

5. After you know which songs produce feelings of well-being, you may want to create an uplifting, energizing playlist, as well as a relaxing, soothing playlist.

❧ WHEN ❧

Use music to quickly induce feelings of calm and peace—especially when transitioning from work to home, or after any stressful or demanding situation.

favorite place 21 visualization

Everyone has a favorite place that produces a smile. Maybe you remember the family vacation you took when you were a child. Perhaps it is a nearby park, a scenic vista point, or special walking trail that you frequent. Your favorite place may be an art gallery, museum, or concert hall that holds special memories. By recalling a favorite place, you drink in the same positive emotions you felt as when you were actually there. Here's how to take an all-expense paid, impromptu trip.

❦ HOW ❦

1. Find any quiet place where you can sit for a minute or two. Decide on a favorite place, making sure it's also a place where you feel safe and secure.

2. In as much detail as possible, picture all the things you enjoy about your favorite locale—the colors, freshness of the air, sounds, sights, and smells.

3. Now, imagine yourself engaging in whatever activity you would normally do in your favorite place, such as walking, hiking, meditating, playing, or just being.

4. Notice if you sense any changes in your body—including deepened breathing, increased heart rate, or slight muscle movements.

5. Consider combining a favorite place with a favorite hobby or activity that gives you energy and makes you feel good. Even if you don't presently participate in that activity, you can still imagine yourself enjoying and engaging in it again.

❦ WHEN ❦

Engage in this visualization any time that you want to get a fresh perspective, feel positive energy, or get motivated and inspired. Also, consider using this during a work break or any time that you need to get mentally refreshed.

22 calming self-hug

We all know that getting a friendly, non-sexual hug can be soothing and uplifting. A hug is an extended pat on the back that sends the message, "you're okay and it feels good to be near you." A self-hug gives you that same message when no one else is around. A self-hug is an antidote for those times you feel lonely and want to feel safe and cared for.

HOW

1. Cup both your hands gently over your heart. Let your hands be soft as you imagine breathing into the heart center.

2. Say the following affirming words:

   I am loved and I value myself. Because I value myself, I promise to take care of myself. I am strong and resilient, and there are others who care about me and love me. I am thankful for what is in my life and will find resources to help me move forward.

3. Holding onto this affirmation, raise your hands high above your head. Then slowly lower your hands in a downward sweeping motion that brings your palms past the front of your face, torso, legs, and finally down to the feet. As the hands move over the body, picture your affirmation being absorbed into your whole being.

4. Now, cross your arms in front of the chest and put each palm on the opposite shoulder to invite inner hospitality with a self-hug.

5. Hold this hug until you feel soothed, calm, and cared for.

WHEN

Enjoy a self-hug anytime you feel lonely or need a reminder that you are capable, loved, and taking care of your needs.

extend the 23
compassionate heart

There is no denying that suffering is part of life. Consider: There is the suffering of being criticized, misunderstood, or unappreciated. Even the wealthy suffer by obsessing about losing wealth and status. Each stage of life has challenges, whether being a teenager, adult, parent, manager, or employee. Though it might appear as if there is no good way to respond to this universal experience, there is one approach: Extend your compassionate heart. While no one has the power to completely eliminate suffering, we can do our best to reduce it. Compassion is a healing salve, a transformative gift of caring and presence that you can offer to yourself and others.

❧ HOW ❧

1. Picture someone from your past or present around whom you have felt safe and loved when in that person's presence. Imagine that grandparent, family member, or friend sending their deep wish for your well-being, happiness, safety, and peace. Bask yourself in this warm, friendly wish for a minute or two.

2. Now, say these words for yourself:

   May I be safe, happy, healthy, peaceful, and at ease.

   May I be free from pain, hunger, and suffering.

3. Finally, extend these same warm, compassionate thoughts outward—even to one who has caused you pain. This is not to excuse another's actions, but just to be compassionate and see through the broader lens of understanding, love, and peace.

❧ WHEN ❧

Use this practice to help you bounce back from disappointment and suffering. Even if you have suffered because of others, this practice may help you experience them with greater openness—and even some understanding for how all beings have endured suffering.

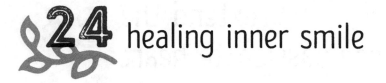# 24 healing inner smile

With so many daily distractions, it's easy to get lost in mental busyness and forget about what is with us all the time—this marvelous body that carries our consciousness and follows our every command so that we can accomplish so much each day. This practice offers a way to connect with, honor, and appreciate the body. In doing so, you tap a deep reservoir of resilience that is sure to recharge your batteries.

✤ HOW ✤

1. Sit, stand, or lie down and close your eyes. Let your mouth and lips form a partial smile, much like the Mona Lisa's soft smile.

2. Bask the entire body in a warm glow of gratitude and appreciation, starting from the feet and up the legs to the torso, arms, back, neck, head, and face.

3. Send the warm glow of appreciation not just onto the surface of the body, but deep, deep into the tissues and all the way down into all your cells.

4. Picture your inner smile comforting the internal organs of the body, such as the liver, kidneys, stomach and intestines, heart, and lungs.

5. Bring your healing smile into the brain itself.

6. Conclude with the intentional wellness statement:

   May my entire body be well, may its healing capabilities work to their full potential, bringing all of the body into harmony and ease as it was intended to be.

✤ WHEN ✤

This is an ideal practice to use in the evening before sleep, as well as any time of the day, or when you are feeling tired, exhausted, or sick.

catch a calm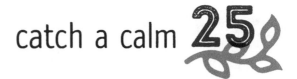

Just as we can "catch a cold" from others, it's easy to catch emotional upset and dis-ease from our surroundings. Catching an emotional cold can come from disturbing violence on the news or being around emotionally negative and reactive persons. Buffering from emotional negativity is vital to maintaining your emotional immune system and defenses. Catching a calm is as refreshing as stepping out of a smoky room to catch a breath of fresh, pure air.

HOW

1. Spend a minute here and there throughout the day to check for symptoms of an emotional cold. If you feel on edge, anxious, or just not like yourself, think back on any situation, person, or event that you came in contact with earlier in the day. If possible, avoid this source of future "colds."

2. Catch a "calm" by reading or watching something with a hopeful, spiritual, or optimistic message.

3. Seek out and spend time with a friend or family member who you know is generally even-keeled and happy.

4. Make a point of doing something nice for someone. Spread goodwill and kindness when you get the opportunity. This will have a positive boomerang effect and help get rid of your cold.

5. Nourish yourself with a cup of tea or coffee, the warmth of the sun, time in nature, and the relationships you hold dear.

WHEN

Taking your daily dose of calm is a powerful way to stay balanced and resilient. The more you do this, the more you will find yourself feeling calm and centered, as well as being able to help others to "catch a calm."

PART 2

clarity

There are a lot of factors that can derail clarity and your
ability to function and maintain resilience at a high level.
By skillfully staying clear, engaged, and present, you
avoid the daily traps that sap your precious energy, focus,
purpose, sense of humor, balance, ability to function
effectively, and self-knowing awareness and insight.
With clarity you bring your best self forward.

the protein brain cure

If you want to have mental and emotional clarity, you need to feed the brain the kind of nutrition that gets its cognitive machinery in gear. There are some easy guidelines for accomplishing this goal. Resilience comes from taking the best possible care of your self, so why not start the first thing in the morning?

✎ HOW ✎

1. Eat a morning meal. No matter how rushed you are in the morning, a cup of coffee by itself, no matter how lovely and satisfying, doesn't qualify as a complete meal.

2. Get some kind of protein in the morning. That's because proteins break down into amino acids, which are used as building blocks for neurotransmitters. Here are some basic guidelines:

   • To strengthen attention and motivation, eat dairy products like milk and yogurt, or nibble on some almonds or sesame seeds. Eat a banana or other fruit.

   • Calm and regulate your moods with foods such as a peanut butter sandwich, turkey, and cottage cheese.

   • Improve thought and memory by eating such foods as eggs, salmon, or a slice of whole wheat bread.

3. Get a serving of protein every two to three hours. This helps the thinking part of the brain focus and concentrate.

✎ WHEN ✎

If it helps, prepare your foods in advance. A hard-boiled egg, for example, is quick and offers you a complete protein. Each time you make the right morning food choices you are increasing your resilience bank, as well as your cognitive abilities.

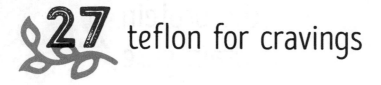 **teflon for cravings**

Cravings and urges are like powerful gusts of wind that can appear quickly and powerfully. If you're not ready, these gusts can spin you out of control and sap your ability to stay on course, not to mention diminish your clarity and resilience. To better manage unexpected (or familiar) cravings, do this:

‿ HOW ‿

1. Get curious about the craving instead of fighting it or giving into it. You can inquire:

   - How intense is this craving?

   - How frequent is this craving?

   - Where is the craving located—is it in the body or is it in the mind?

   - Was there a feeling that preceded this craving—such as loneliness, sadness, abandonment, or boredom, etc.? Give this feeling a name.

   - Does the craving really address the underlying feeling? Or, is it just a temporary escape or distraction from an uncomfortable feeling?

2. Notice and rate the intensity of the craving on a 1-5 scale, with 5 the greatest intensity.

3. Observe and monitor the craving for 1-3 minutes. Notice how the craving is temporary and not permanent, and how its intensity changes over time.

4. Notice how observing and accepting a craving or urge lets you detach from it, even slightly.

5. Now that you have disengaged, consider an alternative choice, behavior, or distraction that turns you away from the craving and toward a more beneficial direction.

‿ WHEN ‿

Become Teflon for cravings whenever you find clarity is being lost due to a craving. This approach lets you outlast the craving, learn more about yourself, and be less vulnerable to unhealthy cravings over time.

change the history channel 28

Does an inner story or movie from your past ever play in your head? This happens to all of us at some point. But if it's an unpleasant and unhelpful movie, or if the inner movie is so vivid and persistent that it keeps you from participating in the moment right before you, then you need to change the channel. The good news? You control the remote.

ᔰ HOW ᔰ

1. Keep track of the number of times you go to the old channel in the course of a day. This helps you recognize the history channel.

2. Each time that you notice the old channel, interrupt it and say to yourself, "It's not me, the just the old channel playing."

3. Turn your attention elsewhere by taking a deep breath, exhaling slowly and stretching your arms and hands outward as if you were pushing the old channel aside.

4. Pay attention to your movements as you mentally or aloud say the words, "I am switching to the present moment channel." (You can even name this channel or station as K-NOW or W-NOW)

5. Refocus your thoughts and attention toward what you were doing before the old channel started playing. Finish changing the channel by stating aloud or mentally, "I have now successfully changed the channel back to the activity of _____."

6. Repeat this as often as needed, regardless of how frequently the old channel keeps popping up.

ᔰ WHEN ᔰ

Change the channel whenever you feel stuck or frustrated by rumination, anxiety, or a negative inner story that keeps repeating. Over time, changing the channel will become easier, so use your remote channel changer as much as needed.

# 29 control the elevator

Humans are emotional beings, and our moods can move up and down throughout the day like an elevator—as external events and individuals push our elevator buttons. But wouldn't it be nice if your elevator didn't automatically go up or down just because someone else pushed a button? While you may not be able to control the external events in your life, you can choose how to react—such as with understanding, amusement, acceptance, equanimity, or wisdom. This practice gives you—the actual elevator operator—a greater understanding and more control over the movement of your emotional elevator.

ஐ HOW ଓଜ

1. Make three columns on a sheet of paper. In the left column, write down a one-sentence snapshot of the external events and persons who operated your mood elevator this past week.

2. In the middle column write down how you reacted and what happened to your mood. Did it go up, down, or remain steady?

3. In the third column, write a sentence describing an alternative perspective or interpretation that you *could have tried* that would have kept your mood steadier.

4. Put the new perspective into action today when a person or situation pushes that same elevator button.

5. Make a mental note of how it feels to operate your own elevator.

ஐ WHEN ଓଜ

Use this practice anytime that you want to feel safe, steady, and more in control upon encountering life's many external button pushers. The more frequently you take charge of your elevator, the more you will gain clarity and resiliency in the face of uncertainty and change.

do the next thing  30

During times of stress and pressure, it's easy to feel overloaded, unfocused, and scattered. At such times you can follow the same advice given to fighter pilots when they face an emergency situation: Do the next thing. In other words, don't worry about what's too far off in the future, but deal with the next thing right before you. As simple as it sounds, it's an effective way to cut problems down to size and sweep away mental clutter.

❧ HOW ❧

1. Break down your goal into its smallest and simplest parts. It doesn't matter if you are shopping for food, cleaning the house, or looking for a job. Write down all the steps required for you to eventually accomplish your goal.

2. Set an amount of time that you will work on the first item on your list. Choose on an amount of time that is realistic and achievable for you.

3. Work on your first item for the allotted time, after which you can either stop or continue on longer. Either way, you have successfully completed this first step for that day.

4. Move on to the second "next thing" on your list. Again, choose how much time you will spend on it at any given time.

5. Go through the list, taking this approach. Remember that doing each next thing in bite-sized pieces is a success and good enough.

❧ WHEN ❧

Use this technique whenever you feel overwhelmed and scattered by too many demands. This practice will help you stay present with the journey, one small step at a time.

 uni-task

Using a cell phone while driving is a good example of how simultaneously doing two things can fracture our attention. Though we're under the illusion that we can do many things at the same time, the thinking brain really does one thing at a time—albeit very quickly. Multi-tasking actually slows you down because it's like losing your place when you are reading. First, you have to remember where you were and find your place before you can resume reading. Training the body and mind to uni-task brings a sense of clarity and accomplishment to whatever you are doing.

❧ HOW ❧

1. Set the intention to do one thing—whether you are talking on the phone, eating, standing, walking, driving, or paying bills. Right now, for example, you can set the intention to read this page without interruption.

2. Follow-up with the action. To devote yourself one hundred percent to the experience of reading, notice how your hands hold the book or electronic device. If your mind wanders, you can refocus on the page by restating your intention of "reading, reading."

3. Observe any distracting thoughts that might pop into your head—or sensations that arise in the body—and then gently let them go so you can return to reading.

4. Practice doing one thing whether you are making a salad, walking, sitting, driving, having a conversation, and so on.

5. When distracted, continue uni-tasking by restating your intention of "walking, walking" or "driving, driving" as you observe the experience of uni-tasking in the body and mind.

❧ WHEN ❧

Use this to stay on task or anytime you are easily distracted and need to regain focus.

be the pebble

Did you ever have so many thoughts swirling around in your head that you almost felt dizzy? Any constant barrage of thoughts can have you white-knuckling it—just as if you were taking a wild river rafting ride. Fortunately, there is a wonderful practice that acts much like dropping a pebble into turbulent water. No matter how choppy or big the waves may be at the surface, the pebble falls harmlessly down to the riverbed where the water is still and quiet. In this way, the pebble (your mind) goes to a quieter and safer place far away from the turbulent thoughts. Here it finds peace, quietude, and stillness.

♾ HOW ♾

1. Find a quiet place where you won't be disturbed and can practice for 1-3 minutes.

2. Pick a neutral word, phrase, or image that won't stimulate more thinking. This can be a soothing word like "calm," "peace," "one," or "pebble," as well as a calming image like the color green, a pebble, or a flower.

3. Favor your chosen "pebble" word, phrase, or image over other thoughts. Don't work too hard at thinking about your word, and it's okay if your thoughts wander. But when you notice your mind is wandering, just gently return to your "pebble."

4. If you have any scary thoughts that won't go away (they usually do), just open your eyes and try this practice another time.

5. Change your posture as needed, being sure to move with awareness.

♾ WHEN ♾

Use this anytime during the day you get a short break and want to quiet and slow down your busy mind.

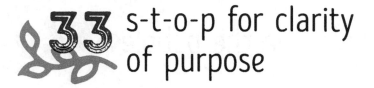# s-t-o-p for clarity of purpose

Did you ever consider how many hundreds of choices you make in the course of a day? It's been estimated, for example, that the average person makes over 200 choices a day just about food. And yet, how many of these choices reflect your deepest values? How many are really connected to your greater purpose? S-T-O-P is an acronym for how to slow down and re-align yourself with what matters in your life. It's ideal when struggling with emotional overload, cravings, fatigue, difficult transitions, or when you feel things are simply moving too fast.

HOW

1. Stand and Slow Down. Take three nice, calming breaths.

2. Tune into the Body. Starting from the feet and moving up the body to the head, locate any tension or tightness in the body, as well as negative emotions. Breathe into areas of tension and then release it as you exhale. Let your thoughts go.

3. Observe Your Surroundings. Using all your senses, identify at least one thing that is novel, pleasant, or soothing in your environment. Or, observe another person with love and understanding.

4. Prepare for Your Purpose. Now that you've slowed things down, what purposeful action can you take that lets you respond thoughtfully—not react impulsively—to the current situation?

5. Follow up on your purposeful choice, whether it is calling a friend for support, getting help, or behaving in a way that is safe, stable, and healthy.

WHEN

Use this portable practice when you are about to enter a stressful situation or after such an event. You can do this almost anywhere and no one will know you are connecting with your purpose.

elevate your view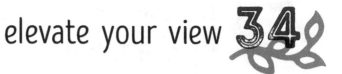

It's all too common to get "stuck in the mud" or entrapped in a mental rut. Sometimes it's not so easy to find a way out of a sticky problem or troublesome emotion. The good news is that you can create space from almost any situation by assuming a more detached and elevated perspective. This allows you to restore resilience and start moving forward in a fresh way.

❧ HOW ❧

1. Picture yourself high on a hilltop, or in a helicopter, looking down on the rut or situation in which you find yourself—whether it is being stuck in traffic or an unsatisfying job.

2. Ask yourself: From my higher viewpoint, what new perspective does this vantage point offer me? This viewpoint might let you see, for example, that you're not alone—that others are stuck in traffic or an unsatisfying job.

3. Take a breather, and take a breath. As you exhale, let go and give yourself a breather, which means time to relax and feel freed from whatever old ideas and emotions that you're holding onto.

4. Recognize that what you're looking at right now—what you're experiencing—is impermanent and temporary. Just as when watching a movie or reading a book, you know that there will be a new scene or chapter. The action you are witnessing at this moment will change in the future.

5. As you watch from above, reflect on another attitude you could take in this moment. How will the next chapter begin?

❧ WHEN ❧

Elevate your view anytime you get caught in a mental rut or find yourself getting too reactive to a situation or person.

35 be the gatekeeper of the mind

Have you ever been lost in thought or fantasy and didn't even know it? This is much like getting on a train and falling asleep. Before you know it, you've missed your stop, and the train is at the end of the line. Staying awake to your thoughts is not always easy, but it is advantageous. It lets you see what your mind is doing, how it reacts, and what it is attracted to or repelled by. Being the gatekeeper of your thoughts is an important training for constructively distancing from thoughts and realizing that they are not necessarily facts.

❧ HOW ❧

1. When you notice your mind is wandering, simply label your thoughts as "mind wandering" or "thinking." This is a neutral way of being a gatekeeper without judging the thoughts—even if they are self-critical ones.

2. When experiencing an emotion, you can also name the emotion. By naming your emotions (see Practice 4, *Calibrate and Tame Your Emotions*), you gain greater fluency and awareness of your feelings.

3. Refocus attention back to the present moment and to whatever you are doing.

4. Repeat this gentle process of labeling your mind-wandering and refocusing attention back to the present.

5. Have patience and self-kindness as you do learn to be the gatekeeper of the mind.

❧ WHEN ❧

Get in the habit of noticing the mind's whereabouts throughout your day. Each time that you catch your thoughts, label your emotions, and refocus on the present, you gain mastery and the resilience needed to stay calm and on course.

mental flossing

Just as the daily build-up of tartar needs to be removed from the teeth by flossing, the build-up of stress due to the day's wear and tear also needs to be cleansed and removed. The practice of mental flossing clears away the accumulation of foggy thinking and mental exhaustion. By mentally flossing, you can be resistant to burnout, irritation, and feelings of isolation.

❧ HOW ☙

1. Morning Time: Stretch when you awaken. Savor taking care of the body, feel the water pulsing on your skin as you shower or bathe. Smell the fresh morning air when you step outside, and appreciate nature's bounty—trees, sky, sun, grass, etc. Finally, think of your day's purpose and how you can manifest this through a single, choice-filled action.

2. Daytime: Make meaningful contact with others—in person, via phone, or via computer. Smile, hug, or share an uplifting story with others. At the very least, hug yourself.

3. Break-Time: Stretch as you listen to music that energizes and soothes your soul. Eat a nourishing snack that you truly enjoy. Have a good laugh about something, anything, by yourself or with others.

4. Evening Time: Reconnect with loved ones. Express your love. Spend time in your garden or cultivating a hobby. Laugh, breathe, and exercise even for a few minutes.

5. Bedtime: Say a prayer, take a handful of meditative breaths, or express gratitude for someone who is in your life.

❧ WHEN ☙

Floss whenever possible. Even taking a moment to breathe deeply is a great mental flossing strategy.

# 37 instant focus booster

There are going to be times during the day when you feel sluggish and lack energy or concentration. Because coffee works best in moderation, you may need another way to shake, rattle, and roll those brain cells awake. Here is an all-natural way to boost your energy and mental focus through breathing. By using this focus boosting practice, you will improve your concentration abilities and feel more awake in just one minute's time.

⤫ HOW ⤬

1. With your fingers clasped together, place your hands firmly under your chin. Coordinating with your breath, you will slowly "flap" your arms up and down like butterfly wings.

2. Inhale deeply on the count of four as you raise your elbows (butterfly wings) upward. Let your chin and head tilt back and upwards as the wings reach their apex. If you feel lightheaded you may be taking too deep a breath. Remember, you don't need to fill up your lungs all the way.

3. Hold your breath for the count of four.

4. Exhale slowly for a count of six as you gradually lower your butterfly wings all the way down. Make sure you let out all the air.

5. Take an additional three or four more focus-boosting butterfly breaths to build up energy.

⤫ WHEN ⤬

Use this focus boosting practice anytime during the day when you feel low in energy, sluggish, or are having a hard time focusing and concentrating on a task.

from anger to heaven 38
in one minute

There's a story about the Samurai warrior who went to see a wise man in order to learn about heaven and hell. The wise sage berated the warrior, saying, "Why would I want to help the likes of you, who thinks so lowly of life that he would harm another?" Incensed and insulted, the warrior raised his sword in anger. "That," said the sage, "is hell." As the truth of the words sunk in, the warrior's demeanor changed and he calmly lowered the blade. "That," said the wise sage, "is heaven." Here's how to find the peace (and a piece) of heaven right now.

HOW

1. Find a quiet place where you can take three long, deep breaths.

2. With each out-breath, visualize your breath carrying the anger down your legs and depositing it out the bottom of your feet and back into the Earth.

3. Imagine you are sitting on the bank of a serene lake, or floating on a boat. The deep blue water is peaceful, calm, still, and cool.

4. Feel a comforting, cool breeze blowing over you, bringing you to a state of peace and calm.

5. Send self-compassion to yourself with these words:

   May I be free from the wheel of suffering that anger produces.

   May all beings be free from this cycle of anger and suffering.

6. Visualize your heart opening, as it grows soft and tender. Feel the peaceful heart, the heart free of pain, anger, and suffering.

WHEN

Tap into heavenly peace and calm whenever you feel upset or about to lose your temper. By seeking heaven inwardly, you create heaven externally.

# stepping off the anxiety train

Thoughts are very much like a train—a train of thoughts so to speak. What happens when you hop aboard a train of anxious thoughts? Where does that train take you? Where is the end of the line? For some, the train carries them to Anxiety Land, Dwellsville, or Panic Town, which are not the most pleasant of locales. This practice can get you off the train and back onto the platform at any time. Even if you did purchase a ticket for this train, you have the power to get off anytime you want—even the next stop.

❧ HOW ❧

1. Be neutral and non-judgmental toward your thoughts. Simply note your anxious thoughts as "mind wandering or "thoughts."

2. Take a stance of openness and acceptance toward the anxiety train. Instead of fighting with your thoughts, greet your train's anxiety conductor with a smile by saying, "Hello again old friend."

3. Appraise your thoughts by looking for evidence. What is the evidence that this thought is *really, honestly accurate?* Is there historical evidence that such thoughts in the past have not been factual? While the fear may *feel* real, the basis of truth on which is it based may not be, and the feeling alone does not make it true.

4. Now that you are on the platform and have gotten off the train, take a nice breath.

5. Smile. Congratulate yourself on getting off the train.

❧ WHEN ❧

Use this any time you feel upset or headed toward unstoppable anxiety or panic. The earlier you can start to get off the anxiety train the easier it will be.

cut the "to-do's" 40
down-to-size

Creating a *To Do* list can have some benefits, but frequently it can produce more angst and worry because the list grows and grows. Before long, you feel like you'll never get it all done. Instead of feeling overwhelmed by your *To Do* list, you can use it to feel good about what you are able to accomplish.

⁓ HOW ⁓

1. Start with a small *To Do* item. Getting a small project out of the way will make you feel good and motivate you to move on to a larger project.

2. Be real. How much time do you really have each day for your list? Set realistic time frames for working on a particular *To Do* project, even if it takes several five or ten minute daily sessions to complete.

3. Uni-task (see Practice 31, *Uni-task,* for a refresher). Turn off the phone and all distractions while doing your projects. This will help you be efficient as you do more in less time.

4. Balance Your Life. Feel good knowing that you don't have to sacrifice your life for a list. The purpose of a *To Do* list is to keep you focused, not to sap the joy out of your day.

5. Find a *To Do* Helper or resource. Get others to help you with your big projects. It can be fun working with others, and you'll get fresh ideas from them.

⁓ WHEN ⁓

Instead of being a slave to your *To Do* list, it is meant to be in service to you. Use this strategy anytime that your *To Do* list creates anxiety for you or you find that you are obsessing over it.

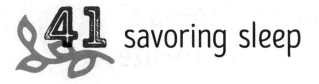# 41 savoring sleep

According to a National Sleep Foundation survey, the average American sleeps fewer than seven hours nightly. That's about one hour less than the recommended average. While everyone requires a different amount of sleep, a sleep deficit can produce problems such as poor memory, difficulty learning, mental fogginess, and unsafe driving. Long-term sleep deficits have been implicated in diabetes, obesity, and weakening of the immune system. If you are sleep-deprived, here are some strategies for making sleep a priority and cutting your sleep debt down to size.

HOW

1. Make your bedroom a technology-free zone. This means removing the TV and electronic devices from your bedroom—including cell phones.

2. Protect your sleep. Set good sleep boundaries by letting others know that you won't accept calls or answer texts and emails after a certain time.

3. Don't get overactive physically right before bedtime. If you need to exercise, do it one or two hours before your bedtime.

4. Consider implementing a sleep ritual (see Chapter 9, *Sleep Ritual*) so that you can have a chill out period that prepares your mind and body for sleep.

5. Affirm a good night's sleep. Set the mental intention before going to bed that you will have a deep and rejuvenating sleep.

6. Upon waking, reaffirm that you had a good night's sleep and that you had enough sleep to function effectively.

WHEN

By using these sleep-enhancing methods each night, you will do more than maximize your sleep. You will maximize your resilience, clarity, and life satisfaction.

body scanning

We live in a very thinking-oriented culture. Sometimes we tend to
forget that the body is just as vitally important, and that mind and body
constantly communicate. This practice helps you drop out of the busy mind
and reconnect with the body. It also strengthens concentration by training
the mind to pay attention to the dynamic nature of the body over and over.

❧ HOW ❧

1. Find a comfortable place to sit, stand, or lie down.

2. Inhale, imagining that your breath can carry your awareness to any part
   of the body, far past the lungs. (Feel free to skip over any part of the body
   where there has been trauma or injury.)

3. Bring the breath and awareness into the left foot. Contact any sensation
   you feel arising, even in the tissue, tendons, ligaments, and bones.

4. After a short time, exhale as you let go of focusing on the foot.

5. Repeat the above process as you move up one side of the body and down
   the other. If desired, combine parts (such as the hip, thigh, knee, calf,
   shin, and ankle). Optionally, you can include internal organs, the skull,
   scalp, face, sense organs, and brain.

6. Lastly, say a blessing of thanks to the body for all it does for you.

❧ WHEN ❧

This is an ideal morning practice because it breaks old morning routines
and makes you more aware of your body's sensations throughout the day. Be
aware that this practice may make you drowsy. If that's the case, however, you
could always use it to help you sleep at night.

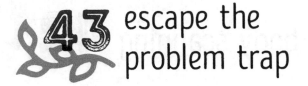

43 escape the problem trap

The Chinese finger trap is a novelty puzzle comprised of a long, flexible, woven tube. After firmly placing a finger from each hand into the ends of the tube, the trick is to free yourself. If you pull too hard, however, the fibers tighten around your fingers like handcuffs. The same is sometimes true of how obsessing on problems can trap us. The secret to getting free from problems that consume you, as with the Chinese finger trap, is to relax rather than tense up. Here's how to let be, get free, and let go.

❧ HOW ❧

1. Worry about your problems with as much energy as you can muster for two minutes and see if it solves anything. Did it? If not, move on to step two.

2. Acknowledge that no one is free of problems and that problems come and go.

3. Accept that your problems are not solvable by tensing up and worrying about them.

4. Take a nice, relaxing breath, and think of a pleasant memory. Notice how nothing changes except that you're more at ease!

5. Make an executive decision to relax and let go of trying to solve your problem for the moment. This does not mean that you are giving up, but that you are wisely opening to a new approach.

6. Set the intention to let your subconscious work on the problem for you—while you take a long walk in nature or at night while sleeping.

❧ WHEN ❧

Use this whenever you can't shut off the mind's obsession with a problem or issue in your life, and you need a breather.

commit to purpose  44

Purpose is the glue that securely attaches a deeper meaning to life. Without purpose, each day would be series of random events. The gift of being human is how we instill life with grace, dignity, and meaning. No one provides you with your purpose. It is something that only you can decipher. It is through purpose that you connect with others and bring goodness into the world.

✌ HOW ✌

1. Choose a guiding purpose that you can focus on for the week. Think of this as a weekly mission statement that describes how you can make a positive difference in some area of your life.

2. On a sheet of paper, write two or three sentences that describe this purpose. This might include being a more attentive parent, a better friend, a more compassionate and understanding boss, a more cooperative employee, or a more loving and respectful spouse.

3. Name one very specific daily action, or behavior, that directly relates to your purpose—such as showing kindness or generosity, listening to your partner without defensiveness, or asking for suggestions from others in the workplace.

4. Journal or share your daily purpose with someone close to you.

5. Feel free to adjust, refine, or change your purpose as fits best with you.

6. Consider writing down a yearly purpose—along with the kinds of specific behaviors that let you know you are accomplishing the longer-term goal you want to reach.

✌ WHEN ✌

Commit to purpose if you feel unsure or unhappy about your current direction. Use this to reinvigorate relationships and help you to move forward in a fulfilling way.

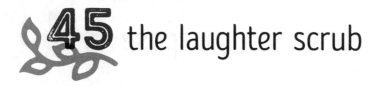# the laughter scrub

Suppose you found an all-natural cure proven to have no side effects that could strengthen your immune system, lower your blood pressure, reduce the risk of heart attack, and scrub out toxic stress hormones from the body. Would you try it? It would probably be worth billions if the pharmaceutical companies could turn it into a pill. But they can't, because the cure is laughter. Laughter has been shown to be effective not just for physical ailments, but as a buffer against depression and an aid for coping with life's difficulties. Here are some quick ways to get the benefits of the laughter scrub.

HOW

1. Call someone who you know makes you laugh or helps you to lighten up. Spend time with this person and see if you can emulate their sense of humor or perspective on things.

2. Make an executive decision to laugh off whatever is causing you unhappy or distressing feelings. No one will do this for you, so you might as well do it.

3. Practice smiling and breathing diaphragmatically at the same time. Start with the sly Mona Lisa smile and let it grow into a full-fledged grin. Or, hold a pencil between your teeth, which creates a smile.

4. Schedule time to watch a funny movie, TV program, or cartoon.

5. Recall a favorite laughter memory, as well as create a new laughter memory for each day. Journal your laughter stories so you can review them and share them with others.

WHEN

Use the laughter scrub whenever you need an emotional pick-me-up. Laughter and anger are not compatible feelings, so it's good to laugh when you are upset or angry.

lean into this moment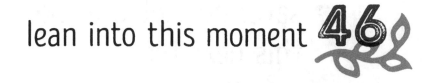

There are an infinite number of ways to use the breath to increase focus and concentration. One technique that is particularly effective, and is even used in some monastic settings, is that of combining the breath with counting. This is helpful for a couple of reasons. Firstly, it gives you immediate feedback as to how tired or unfocused you may be—which you'll quickly discover should you only be able to count to three before losing track. Secondly, it gets you present as it regulates and balances the brain, body, and emotions. It's like an instant tune-up for your vehicle of consciousness, one that will get you up and running smoothly.

❧ HOW ❧

1. Sit, stand, or lie down for this portable practice. Time yourself for one minute.

2. Count each breath you take, starting with number one on the first in-breath, number two on the next in-breath, and so on.

3. Use diaphragmatic breathing (see Practice 1, *Reboot Your Brain with This Precious Breath*).

4. If you lose track of the number at any time, that's okay. Just start at number one again on the next breath.

5. At the end of the minute, see how many breaths you took.

6. Continue for another minute, or longer, if desired. Experiment and see if you can count up to 25 without losing track or getting distracted.

❧ WHEN ❧

This is an excellent practice for those times that you feel out of sorts, mentally hazy, or not really present and focused. If you really need a mental jumpstart, combine this practice with Practice 37, *Instant Focus Booster*.

47 savoring, not grazing, this next bite

One of the obstacles to mindfully eating and savoring food is the tendency to constantly eat, or graze, without really tasting. Changing habits like grazing requires full awareness and a new, healthier practice to substitute for the old one. By savoring, you'll get in the practice of being fully present with each bite—eating what you need, when you need it.

HOW

1. Remove all distractions and turn off technology.

2. Mentally rehearse eating your next snack or meal for one minute. In as much detail as possible, picture yourself eating in a slow, graceful, and dignified way. Taste and smell the food. Imagine the texture as you chew and what it feels like as you swallow. Visualize leaving some food on the plate—even a small amount—as you finish feeling completely full and satisfied.

3. Now, spend one-minute eating mindfully—just as you did in your mental rehearsal. Even if you only take one or two bites in this minute, that's fine.

4. Put down the utensil or food.

5. Pause for a breath. Take this moment to savor the flavor still remaining in the mouth.

6. Complete your meal slowly and mindfully. When done, go to another room for a cup of tea or take a brief walk. This transition lets your body know that this meal is over and you don't need to graze anymore.

WHEN

Do this to start a mindful eating practice. Should you feel the need for a more balanced relationship with food, eating, body, and weight, visit www. mindfulpractices.com for information on the *12-Weeks to Mindful Eating* program and guide.

be a fantasy catcher

Fantasies can be fascinating and fun to indulge in. While some fantasies deliver flights of creativity and represent positive life passions, desires, and hopes, others act as means of escaping into the "what if" rather than facing the "what is" of life. By embodying the "what is," you are more prepared to face the truth of your situation. No matter how stuck or unhappy you feel right now, there is no better place from which to begin the journey forward.

❧ HOW ❧

1. Set the intention to catch your fantasies for a single day.

2. Each time you catch a fantasy, log it onto a sheet of paper.

3. Do not judge a fantasy as good or bad. You are just exploring.

4. Look over your list at the end of the day and ask yourself:

   • Which fantasies repeated most frequently?

   • Was there a major theme—like taking a vacation or finding a new job or relationship?

   • Which fantasies were helpful or insightful? Which were unproductive or unhelpful?

   • What did I learn about myself by being a fantasy catcher?

5. If you are unsure, upset, or disturbed by your fantasies, consider sharing your concerns with a counselor or someone trustworthy who can treat this as confidential.

❧ WHEN ❧

Be a fantasy catcher if you too easily get distracted by unproductive fantasy, or just want to understand your inner world. Being a fantasy catcher might help you recognize important life needs that you've been neglecting. Or, it might help you to escape into fantasy less and live more in the "what is" so you can better deal with real-life issues.

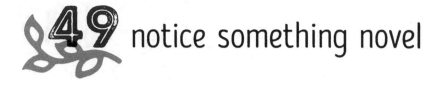

49 notice something novel

We've all driven the same route to work, walked the same path around our neighborhoods or hallways at home or the office. After numerous trips around the same block, we might conclude that there's nothing new to see. But that conclusion is due to the fact that we're probably not paying close enough attention. After all, there's always something new occurring. This practice sweeps away mental cobwebs and gets you off autopilot. When you really want to take a fresh look at the people and places you encounter, try this:

℘ HOW ℘

1. Mentally erase your old mindset. Begin by wiping off your mental chalkboard to clean off old, entrenched beliefs, biases, and opinions about what you see.

2. Create a fresh mindset. Do this by imagining that this is the first time you are seeing a place (freeway, neighborhood, or workplace, etc.) or meeting the person before you (partner, co-worker, friend, etc.), or engaging in an activity.

3. Feel the excitement of someone traveling to a new country or unexplored location. Allow yourself to feel the wonder and spaciousness that comes from exploring and seeing something for the first time.

4. Notice, learn, or experience one novel thing that you discover about this "new" exotic place or person before, whether large or small.

5. What would you tell the people "back home" about your interesting travels?

6. Take a mental snapshot or actual photo of something beautiful, pleasant, or exciting from your day.

℘ WHEN ℘

Use this when things feel humdrum, dull, and repetitive, and you need to reenergize. Getting a fresh mindset is key to remaining alive and resilient.

devoted 100% to 50 this experience

How often have you wished things were different? Did you ever want to be with a different person than the one who was right before you? Did you ever go to dinner with a friend and wished you had ordered the meal your companion was eating? It's easy to reject the "meal" or experience that is right before us—believing that things would be better elsewhere. But did you ever consider: All that happens when you reject this moment is that you end up being unhappy, dissatisfied, and miserable. You can put energy into fighting this moment or you can accept it. That's your choice.

❧ HOW ❧

1. Devote yourself to fully doing just this one thing before you. If you feel resistance toward what you're doing, notice the resistance. How would an attitude of acceptance alter your experience?

2. Set boundaries. Give yourself time to be present by removing distractions and even technology that weaken your commitment to do this one thing.

3. Notice how each sense organ responds as you do your one thing. Notice each touch, sight, sound, smell, etc.

4. Bring back the wandering mind. Each time the mind wanders, bring it back by restating what you are doing, such as, "walking, walking," or "working on project, working on project."

5. Move deliberately and purposefully as you do your one thing.

6. See the sacredness in your one thing. Each ordinary and mundane act, when done with care and attention can be viewed as extraordinary and sacred.

❧ WHEN ❧

Use this practice whenever you feel bored or lose your zest for what you are doing. This is a practice that awakens as it brings meaning to even the most ordinary daily chore or task.

optimism

Optimism makes hope possible. It's the essential attitude by which you can turn those proverbial lemons into lemonade. Optimism is vital to resiliency because it allows you to avoid rigid thinking and to maintain flexibility and adaptability. Optimism, like a well-tuned engine, provides you with the power, energy, and traction needed to bounce back and start moving again when things aren't going your way.

name that strength 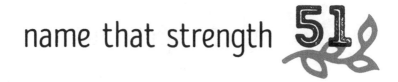 51

Did you ever keep track of how many personal character strengths you exhibit in the course of a day? Very few of us do this. But if you did, you'd start to understand, appreciate, and marvel at how many different positive approaches to life you apply and cultivate on a daily basis. If you've ever said, "I can't," then recognizing and expressing your strengths is the equivalent of saying, "I can."

✎ HOW ✎

1. Identify one of your character strengths. This can be a strength you have noticed or that others have appreciated and identified in you. To look at a list of strengths, visit www.viacharacter.org the non-profit website. It only takes 15 minutes to take their free strengths inventory.

2. Focus on applying one of your strengths in the course of the day. If your strength is kindness, smile or show someone that you care; if humor, share a joke or funny story with another; if perseverance, put in some work toward a long-term goal; if leadership, solicit ideas from others or read about a favorite leader you admire.

3. At the end of the day, write down how you used your strength and how this made you feel.

4. Continue using your strength every day for a week.

5. At the end of the week, reflect on how working on your strength improved your mood or helped you accomplish more and be more effective.

6. Choose a new strength for the following week.

✎ WHEN ✎

Use this to feel more optimistic about yourself, as well as to accurately to affirm, recognize, and put your best qualities to work.

# 52 b.l.i.s.s. practice

Have you ever witnessed a view of nature so extraordinary—like the jaw-dropping vistas of the Grand Canyon—that you experienced a state of bliss? It's hard not to experience a deep sense of joy and optimism in such moments. Fortunately, you don't have to travel hundreds of miles to experience bliss. With the B.L.I.S.S. practice you don't even need to leave your own backyard.

❧ HOW ❧

1. **B**e in your body. Take a deep breath. Let the body settle until it is rooted, stable and secure—whether you are seated, standing, or lying down. Come to rest and find your center.

2. **L**isten with love. Open and become receptive. Let the warmth of your heart radiate through the whole body, and saturate all your cells with light and love. Let yourself soften with compassion and understanding for yourself and all beings.

3. **I**magine a peaceful healing symbol or image. This could be a loved one, a spiritual image, a rainbow, or a hiking trail.

4. **S**ense your body. Perceive the body within as you notice any changing feelings or images. Sense the body's wisdom, neither forcing nor judging. Just sense the calm of the peaceful image within your body.

5. **S**ense the sacred. Feel a sense of the sacred both within and surrounding you. Expand your gaze, letting it penetrate the beauty and preciousness of all things that grace your space, life, and world.

❧ WHEN ❧

Use this practice whenever you need to give your spirit a lift. Try it after a long day at work or anytime you feel physically or mentally weary.

imagine your 53
joyful future self

What if you could feel better about the future just by thinking about it? There's evidence that this is possible, and several studies have shown that visualizing a successful future can impact feelings of optimism, happiness, hope, and even serve to develop coping skills. It only takes a few minutes to envision a joyful future that you can make happen.

✌ HOW ✌

1. Locate and connect with feelings of joy. Do this by thinking about a time you felt joyful or were passionate about something.

2. Visualize how you looked and felt at that joyful time. Feel the hope and optimism that you felt. What does this feel like in your body? If negative thoughts creep in, notice these with a sense of acceptance but without identifying with them. Return to the feelings of joy.

3. Maintaining your feeling of joy, imagine what your joyful future self might look like in one, five, or ten years. (If desired, set the intention to imagine how joy could lead you toward a realistic goal, personal potential, or a life dream.) Remember— your future self is an expression of the joy you feel *now*. Don't get too attached to a future outcome.

4. For up to five minutes, visualize, then write the story of how joy moved you forward. What strengths helped you on your journey to your future?

5. Each week, re-visualize how joy can move you forward.

✌ WHEN ✌

Imagine your joyful future self when you want a clearer picture of how to reach your desired and meaningful future. If you're stuck or frustrated, this will get you excited, optimistic, and energized again.

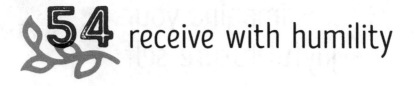# 54 receive with humility

Did you ever have a hard time asking for help? In our independent-oriented and "I can do all of it by myself" culture, receiving assistance can be viewed negatively. Knowing how to ask for help is not a weakness, but a sign of strength that allows us to connect with others. In truth, giving would not be possible without a receiver. Opening to help from others teaches us the importance of humility as you build relationships by tapping the wealth of resources that surround you.

HOW

1. Reflect on how no one really does it alone. To think otherwise is just an illusion. We need each other to maintain our basic needs, including food, shelter, roads to drive on, electricity, and so on.

2. Identify what you need help with. Be honest, even if it is difficult. Whether you need food, a tutor, a mentor, help with a business plan, find someone who has expertise in that area.

3. Write down a list of up to three persons who you trust and have the expertise to help you, give good advice, and can locate other necessary resources.

4. Research for useful social resources and services.

5. Contact all your resources.

6. Be direct in asking for what you need. Do not apologize for asking for help.

7. Express your sincere gratitude and appreciation for the help you receive.

WHEN

Experience the optimism that comes from solving problems and getting help when you have hit that brick wall, or when you could use a fresh perspective or guidance.

let go of grasping  55

Did you ever get so fixated on wanting something that you suffered because of it? Did you ever become obsessed with getting that new car, house, or perfect relationship? But what if, instead of believing that only that special car or job will make you happy, you just preferred it? By simply preferring something, you soften and open up to other possibilities instead of grasping at just one outcome that you must have.

✁ HOW ✁

1. Identify what it is that you are grabbing onto too tightly.

2. Clench your hands and make two fists. Tighten your hands and fists, imagining that you are holding onto that thing that you want so badly. Notice the tension, tightness, and discomfort.

3. Take a breath in, and as you exhale, release your hands from grasping and holding. Let the blood and circulation return to your fingers. Shake your hands, letting them grow flexible and soft. This is what it is like to let go of unhealthy grasping and an obsessive need.

4. Imagine yourself releasing your attachment, as you open to new and alternative possibilities and preferences.

5. Feel how pleasant and liberating it is to be soft, receptive, and open, without the rigid demands and pain caused by grasping.

6. Spend a moment appreciating what is already in your life.

✁ WHEN ✁

Release grasping and attachment you notice yourself obsessing on the object of your desire, losing sight of the bigger picture, or when you are rigidly stuck to a particular outcome or goal. Now is the time to open up to all the available potential that exists.

 # 56 appreciate the glass

It has been said that the difference between a pessimist and an optimist is that one sees the glass as half-empty while the other sees it as half-full. Which one is more accurate? Actually, anything can be viewed from multiple perspectives. Another point of view is to simply learn to appreciate the "glass"—however you tend to view it. Optimism grows when we can appreciate things as they are. Maybe the glass is good enough as is for now. Maybe it offers you a valuable place from which to cultivate positive feelings about the fact that your "glass" is not all you had hoped or expected it to be.

❧ HOW ☙

1. Identify a situation in your life that you are having trouble accepting—that boss who makes your life miserable, the debt and bills you face, etc.

2. Use mental jujitsu to flip the situation you seek to reject—transforming it into appreciation. For example, how could you envision your "glass" as a gift—something you could be grateful for?

3. Accept how everyone has a different "glass" to deal with. Your situation is something from which you can grow and learn.

4. List the skills and strengths that you can use to continue going forward.

5. Name one thing you can learn—about yourself or others—from seeing your "glass" in a new, expansive and more appreciative way.

❧ WHEN ☙

Use your strength and skill of appreciation if you find yourself being pessimistic about your life and are steeped in negativity. Appreciation changes your view by letting you see things through a more optimistic and resilient lens.

build trust 57
with mutuality

No relationship starts off with instant trust. Trust is something that is gained and earned through each interaction. It is built piece by piece on the building blocks of mutuality through shared interests, reciprocation, cooperation, respect, and a willingness to listen and understand each other. Mutuality means taking a real interest in what another has to offer. It allows you to create a bridge, even with that difficult person in your life. And if your mutuality is not returned?—you have still offered a kind gift of understanding.

❧ HOW ❧

1. Be attentive and listen with respect. Give the one in front of you your full and undivided attention. Set aside technology and avoid other distractions.

2. Let go of your own agenda for the moment. You can always return to your old viewpoint later, but for now, allow yourself to be open and free of judgment and personal bias.

3. Align with an open body posture and gestures. Take a non-defensive body posture, such as not crossing your arms over your chest. Let your gestures be safe and non-threatening. Make appropriate eye contact.

4. Be curious. Don't interrupt, but ask clarifying questions like a detective who wants to know more.

5. Empathize. Imagine putting yourself in the shoes of another. Let yourself feel what it would be like to share in another's experience.

6. Show you care. Take an active interest in the ideas, hobbies, and life of the person you are spending time with.

❧ WHEN ❧

Use this practice when you want to improve communication skills, build intimacy, and feel more optimistic about your relationships.

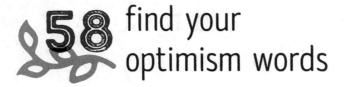

58 find your optimism words

The words you tell yourself have a lot to do with shaping your inner mental landscape. Even the Navy SEALs, for example, train their recruits to challenge inner negative self-talk with positive "can do" thoughts. How optimistic is your thinking? Does your mind throw up a mental roadblock before you even take action? Finding and using an optimistic internal and external vocabulary can add to how resilient you feel each day.

HOW

1. Make a list of words or phrases that imply or generate optimism—such as *I can, I will, can do, anything's possible, potential, possibility, doable, fascinating, positively, upbeat, uplifting, hopeful, affirming, rewarding, opportunity, that's great, awesome, amazing, incredible, achievable, favorable, another chance, and astounding.*

2. Use as many of your optimism-generating words throughout the day as you can. Count each time you use such a word.

3. When you find that you have had a mindless negative or pessimistic thought or said something that is not optimistic or positive, replace it with a more optimistic word or throught on the spot.

4. Reflect on how using an optimistic vocabulary affects your mood and/or behavior. Even if it feels foreign to act with optimism, give it a try.

5. Congratulations on expanding your vocabulary. The point of this practice is not to be phony with optimism, but to acknowledge that thoughts you have can affect how you feel, which in turn can affect how you behave.

WHEN

Use this throughout the day, or anytime when you want to overcome fear, worry, and negativity that might be holding you back.

wisdom of perhaps 59

There was once a bank teller named Bob who lost his job at a bank due to downsizing. When his neighbor found out, the neighbor said, "That's really bad luck." "Perhaps," answered Bob. The very next day while taking a walk, Bob ran into an old friend—who worked for a different bank. After hearing Bob's story, the friend told Bob about a new job opening. Bob landed a much better job, and when his neighbor found out, he exclaimed, "That's great. You're so lucky!" Again, Bob answered, "Perhaps." As smart as we humans are, we are not terribly accurate when it comes to predicting the future. The wisdom of "perhaps" offers another path.

❧ HOW ❧

1. Look at your assumptions when faced with a negative situation or loss. What are your predictions? Do you tend to expect things to turn out a certain way?

2. Examine the facts. Has a loss or negative situation of some kind—such as losing a friend, losing a job, getting a bad grade, or getting rejected for a loan—ever resulted in something positive that you couldn't have anticipated?

3. Let go of your bias and prediction about what you believe will happen next.

4. Embrace the attitude of "perhaps." By taking a more balanced, open, and neutral attitude of "perhaps," you are not predisposing yourself toward a particular outcome that might cause you to become emotionally out of balance or reactive.

❧ WHEN ❧

Use the "perhaps" perspective when an unexpected or unwanted event or loss occurs. This will help you remain resolute, steady, and keep your resilience intact.

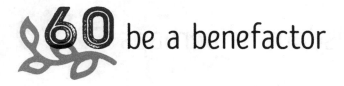# 60 be a benefactor

There is probably no better way to experience and spread optimism than by acting as a benefactor for another. A benefactor is someone who gives hope, good advice, a helping hand, or just makes you feel good and completely accepted when you are in their presence. Benefactors come from any walk of life. It might be that stranger who fixed your flat tire, a grandparent or family member, the kind teacher who took you under his or her wing, and that loyal friend who was always there for you. As a benefactor, you enrich others and yourself by spreading joy and optimism.

১৯০ HOW ৩৩

1. Set the intention to act as a benefactor. Your intention can be for today, for the week, or a long-term commitment for an organization.

2. Identify your gift. Your gift is whatever you have to offer—your special expertise or experience, your kindness, altruism, a smile. The ability to volunteer or donate materially can be your gift.

3. Be prepared to act. You never know when your ability to act as a benefactor will be called upon. One woman, for example, periodically bought plants for strangers at the local nursery—and she considered this form of giving as central to her spiritual path. There is no limit to when and how you can serve as a benefactor.

4. One kindness is good enough. Being a benefactor doesn't mean you have to change the world. Doing one small good, kind, decent thing is both meaningful and important.

১৯০ WHEN ৩৩

Make this a daily practice and you will uplift your mood, feel connected to others, and share of yourself.

take a mental vacation

It only takes a few moments to rejuvenate your self with a mental vacation. Research has shown that when you vividly picture yourself doing something with a mental rehearsal, your brain responds as if you are actually experiencing that event. This practice has been used to improve the performance of athletes, so why not take a relaxing and rejuvenating vacation in your mind to regain your resilience?

❧ HOW ☙

1. Find a quiet place where you won't be disturbed.

2. Recall a vacation, place, or time when you felt at ease, relaxed, and rejuvenated.

3. Close your eyes and vividly picture the place where you took your vacation. See it in as much detail as possible, using all your senses. If it was at the beach, for example, let yourself smell the ocean breeze, hear the ocean surf tumbling onto the shoreline, feel the warmth of the sun on your body and the sand on your feet, and smell the scent of the fresh air or tanning lotion.

4. If you are participating in an activity during your visualization, such as swimming, surfing, hiking, skiing, etc., visualize your movements and surroundings.

5. Continue your visualization for one to two minutes.

6. Notice any changes in your body—breathing, movement, energy, and respiration—that correspond with your visualization. Even as you open your eyes, let yourself continue to bask in the good feelings and rejuvenation that this mental vacation brings. Carry it with you, feeling refreshed as you continue with your day.

❧ WHEN ☙

Take a quick mental vacation whenever you feel worn out, unproductive, uncreative, and uninspired.

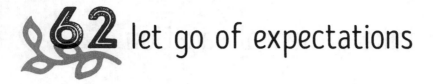62 let go of expectations

What would your life be like if you changed your expectations, lowered them, or even stopped letting them determine how you reacted? Behind expectations there may be lurking a rigid "should" belief or rule about the way things are supposed to be. And yet, "shoulds" often make life more difficult, causing us to harshly judge others—and often ourselves. By letting go of rigid expectations, you can be more flexible, adaptable, and accepting of what's out of your control.

ཤྩ HOW ଦ

1. Name one expectation that gets you upset. Is it when someone doesn't text you right back or say "excuse me" after bumping into you, or doesn't do his or her job as well as you? Or, maybe there's a personal expectation like getting the best review at work or throwing that perfect "Martha Stewart" party. The list is endless.

2. Make an executive decision to let go of your expectation for an afternoon, an hour, or the entire day. You can always return to it later if you want.

3. Choose to adopt a stance of openness and acceptance towards this expectation. Think of it as your preference instead of a "should."

4. Ask yourself, "Realistically, what's the worst thing that could happen in the next five minutes if this expectation is not met?"

5. Respond differently. Choose a behavior that takes you off auto-pilot and lets you respond in a flexible and adaptable way.

6. Think of one benefit of loosening up on your expectations.

ཤྩ WHEN ଦ

Let go of expectations when you are too hard on yourself, react negatively too quickly, or when you need an emotional chilling.

remember a 63
positive outcome

When things aren't going our way, it's easy to feel stuck and lose resiliency. Positivity breeds positivity. And so, when we're feeling down or have lost our zest and energy, recalling a successful and positive outcome from the past might be just what the doctor ordered to shift your mood and energy in a helpful direction. Remembering and relishing a positive outcome from your past is not self-centeredness or bragging. Rather, it's a useful reminder of how the big wheel of life constantly turns, and that change is inevitable.

❧ HOW ☙

1. Get settled in a quiet place and take three calming breaths.

2. Recall any situation where you enjoyed a positive outcome. This can be similar or different from the situation you now find yourself in.

3. Recall your positive outcome in as much detail as you can. This could be anything from a positive relationship outcome to being proud of an accomplishment or reaching a material goal.

4. Remind yourself that things always change, just like the weather. The secret is in knowing that the clouds will eventually clear away and the sun will shine again.

5. Locate a coping skill. While steeping yourself in your positive outcome, do you recognize any skill that helped you reach your positive outcome? Is that skill applicable here and now?

6. Appreciate your resilience. Above all, appreciate the strengths and resources you have applied in your life. These are the keys to getting unstuck and moving forward.

❧ WHEN ☙

Use the practice of remembering a positive outcome any time that you feel stuck and would benefit from a resilience booster of confidence and positivity.

 **friends for boosting optimism**

Take a few seconds to reflect on how the moods of others are contagious—particularly negative ones. Fortunately, just as you can "catch a calm" from others (see Practice 25), you can just as easily catch the optimism bug. Optimistic friends remind us about the nice, good, and beautiful things in life. They know how to find these things, and they can help you find them too.

ᲛᲞ HOW ᲛᲞ

1. Identify someone in your life who can serve as your Optimism Resource Person, or ORP. This can be a friend, family member, or associate.

2. Verify this is an ORP. Usually, it feels good being around an ORP. This is someone who always looks for the possibilities, not for what is lacking. Instead of waiting in the complaint line at a store, they'd try to find the gratitude line.

3. Arrange to spend time with your ORP. In person would be good, but a phone conversation can work.

4. Follow your ORP's lead. Make a commitment to yourself not to drift into complaint or negativity. Let the ORP lead the conversation.

5. Learn from your ORP. Make a mental note of how the ORP maintains an optimistic outlook—especially when facing difficult situations or life challenges. How does their optimistic attitude help them?

6. Model being an ORP for another friend. See how this changes the experience with that friend and how it makes you feel to filter experience through the lens of an ORP.

ᲛᲞ WHEN ᲛᲞ

Use this when you need a lift, a laugh, or a fresh perspective on how to invite optimism into your day.

grow your relationships

Relationships aren't manufactured, but are cultivated and grown through each nurturing gesture, kindness, and act of generosity. Even a drooping plant perks up with a few drops of fresh rain. It is possible to nourish most relationships, even those in disrepair. Now is the time to start growing your relationships so you can enjoy the fruits of togetherness, optimism, and resilience that are sure to follow.

HOW

1. Do one thoughtful and kind thing for your friend. For example, write a short note of thanks or appreciation for the friendship. Always tell your friend know how much you enjoyed visiting. Surprise your friend with a small token of appreciation—something you know he or she will enjoy. In these ways you give your emotional generosity. Emotions are the nutrients that relationships need to thrive.

2. Be present and respectful. When with your friend, remove as many distractions as possible. If you are eating with a friend, for example, put your phone on vibrate and do not answer it.

3. Reciprocate and be mutual. You may have the most fascinating and exciting life on the planet, but you need to ask about your friend and show that you are interested and care.

4. Listen to your friend with empathy and understanding—and without trying to judge or change them.

5. Give of your time. Give of your time when your friend is in need. Making time to be together—face-to-face if possible—is a good first step.

WHEN

Grow your relationships every day, because caring relationships will enliven and enlighten your life in ways that money can't buy.

66 the optimist's breath and body

Have you ever noticed your body posture when you are feeling down or on edge? When an individual feels down, that person's gaze is often focused downward. And when someone feels edgy or upset, that person's muscles—in the jaw, hands, and shoulders—often tense up. Conversely, by changing your posture, you can bring the body and mind into an optimistic unison.

❧ HOW ☙

1. Find an open, quiet place big enough for you to stretch your arms out wide. If you can do this outside that would be ideal.

2. Start with a smile. Even if you don't feel it, fake it until you make it, smiling during this exercise.

3. Take a nice, long in-breath as you picture yourself inhaling all the good and beauty that exists. Take in the kindnesses, the beauty of nature, and the advantages of the man-made world. Let this goodness seep into your cells.

4. Exhale, feeling relaxed and soothed.

5. For the second breath, spread your arms out in front of you and to your sides, as if you are preparing to give someone a hug. This gesture is one of receiving, so see yourself opening up to, and receiving, all the goodness that is available to you. Remain open like this for up to four seconds.

6. Exhale and bring your hands to your heart center, palms touching. Remain like this for a few more moments, letting optimism continue to flow within you with each new breath.

❧ WHEN ☙

Use this breath and body movement practice to dramatically shift toward optimism in the morning or during any transitional or chaotic period.

cross the threshold 67
into kindness

Each time that you move between rooms or spaces, even into and out of your car, you cross a threshold. How present are you to all the thresholds you pass through in an average day? These include such things as stepping into a new room, stepping off the curb, crossing from one side of the street to the other, going from inside to outside, moving up and down in an elevator, waking up from sleep, and so on. Awakening to each new threshold can get you off autopilot and engage you fully in each new moment.

ᔆᔆ HOW ᔆᔆ

1. Identify and become aware of the many thresholds around you. Thresholds are not just identified by doorways, even windows can be a visual threshold to the outside and nature. Mealtime is a threshold that takes you from a place of hunger to feeling satiated.

2. Ask yourself, "Do I respond to any threshold in an autopilot way?" For example, how do certain thresholds affect how you feel—such as the threshold of the on-ramp of a congested freeway?

3. Do the following when stepping over the next threshold:

   • Pause as you prepare to step over the threshold.

   • Take a long, calming breath.

   • Take off the old filters and let yourself enter this new space awakened and without being on autopilot.

4. Set the following intention:

   In the next one-minute,

   As I step through each new threshold,

   May I bring awareness, kindness and compassion with me.

ᔆᔆ WHEN ᔆᔆ

Try this practice when you want to break habitual behaviors, as well as stop frequent worrying about the future or past.

68 overcome procrastination with purpose

Procrastination can take the air out of anyone's balloon, quickly deflating optimism. One of the best medicines for treating procrastination is purpose. Purpose can instill any activity—including the less than exciting ones—with a sense of meaning. Even walking your dog because you care about your pet is a nice way of blending purpose with getting physical exercise. Purpose is very personal, so connect with whatever motivates you the most.

❧ HOW ☙

1. Identify the activity that you are procrastinating with or delaying.

2. Write a purpose list. What do you care about? Who or what matters?

3. Match a purpose with the activity you need to do. Think about a purpose that would motivate you enough to get engaged. Doing chores, such as laundry, may not be appealing, but if your purpose is to care for yourself and your family, that might help you to get started.

4. Start small. Set a time limit for your activity. Even one minute is enough time to get started working on any activity. You can always go for a longer period of time if you want. However much you finish, you can consider it to be a partial success.

5. If the purpose you assign doesn't initially help, try another one or recall a purpose that has motivated you in the past. Don't feel stuck to a particular purpose.

6. Make a note of how it feels when you bring purpose to an activity. How does the body feel? Do you have more energy?

❧ WHEN ☙

Link your purpose to any activity in order to get you moving forward or when you need motivation.

nothing but the facts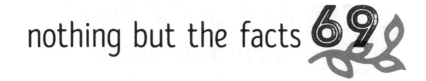

Detectives are known for looking at the cold hard facts of a case. Letting their emotions get in the way won't do. Powerful emotions can cloud our thinking, making it difficult to get the whole story. Though we might have very specific emotions or thoughts about a particular event, these are not necessarily facts. Sometimes it's vital to look for evidence in order to find a more balanced and optimistic viewpoint.

ஒ HOW ௧

1. Write down a snapshot of your situation. In no more than a sentence, write down what's happening. For example: "I'm afraid to ask for a raise."

2. Write down all the emotions that you feel in your situation. Circle the emotion that you feel most intensely, such as "fear."

3. Using that circled word, write down a belief that uses this word. For example, that might be, "I fear I'll lose my job if I ask for a raise," or "I fear I'm not good enough to merit a raise."

4. Write down evidence that challenges, or refutes this belief. For example, evidence might be, "I've always gotten good reviews at work," or "I know others who asked for raises and got them." This evidence gives you the bigger picture.

5. On an index card, write your persistent fear on one side and the bigger picture evidence statement on the other.

6. Carry this card (or put this on your smart phone) with you to challenge your negative thoughts with evidence.

ஒ WHEN ௧

Use this to counter a persistent negative thought or emotion. By coming up with evidence you can challenge erroneous thoughts whenever they appear.

70 go with the flow to open new doors

Experienced swimmers know better than to fight riptides that can pull them out to sea. Instead, they go with the flow until the riptide's grip lessens. Then, they can use their energy to swim back to shore. If you feel like you are swimming against the tide and nothing is working, then you may need to put things in neutral and let yourself go with the flow.

HOW

1. Identify what hasn't been working. It can be anything from trying to stay with an unsatisfying job to a frustrated attempt to attain that dream house.

2. Put your desires in neutral. Let go of trying to force things in a certain direction.

3. Reframe your desire from the grasping place of "I must have" to the more relaxed and spacious place of "it would be nice to have."

4. Imagine yourself being in the flow and not being tied to your previous need or fixed desire.

5. Close your eyes and visualize yourself flowing down a stream. Let yourself move freely, not constrained by what you see or feel. What images appear to you? What do you feel?

6. Use this flowing visualization again if you don't experience anything the first time. Eventually, you may get ideas about other doors that will freely open for you. These new paths may be the fulfilling ones that have been there all the time—just waiting for you to let go of the old ones.

WHEN

When the door you keep knocking on refuses to open, experiment with this practice to let loose and become excited and optimistic about new possibilities.

contact the wise one within 71

With so many daily pressures and demands, it's not uncommon to feel confounded, confused, and foggy. When this happens, we may feel unanchored, like a ship drifting and directionless. As a result, our confidence, self-trust and self-reliance get dinged, and we become far less resilient and less certain about what to do. There is, however, a way to counter confusion by tapping into the wellspring of profound wisdom that resides within you at all times.

✤ HOW ✤

1. Pause and slow down. Find a place to sit and be present.

2. Take three calming breaths.

3. Set the following intention: "May I contact my wise and nurturing self."

4. Imagine yourself five or ten years in the future—having the clarity and perspective of those additional years, and the wisdom that comes along with that. Know that this part of you has your best interests at heart.

5. Ask your future nurturing, mothering, and wise self about your current situation. Without expectation, open yourself to the wisdom within. Try not to judge as you notice any images you see, feelings in the body, words you may hear.

6. Don't force any answers. You may need to contact your wise, nurturing self more than once. Sit with whatever your experience is, sensing how this wisdom feels for you. What would be required for you to embrace it?

✤ WHEN ✤

Witness your wise and nurturing self if you lack confidence and are unsure about important decisions you need to make. Check in with your wise self for guidance as frequently as needed to reaffirm a direction in your life that will bring newfound hope and optimism.

72 conquer fear and feel alive

The ancient, risk-averse part of the brain is always online. Like a smoke detector, it is looking for any wisp of smoke, and is ready to warn you of any potential threat. That's all great, except how do you know when your "smoke detector" is too sensitive? If it is too easily activated, you may be holding back from the joy of this moment and the true experience of aliveness. Sometimes, you need to manually override the automatic smoke detector.

❧ HOW ❧

1. What would you like to do, but avoid doing because of worry or fear? Write this down—whether it's meeting new people, going on a date, strolling a new neighborhood, trying a new food, riding in a hot air balloon, or going on vacation by yourself.

2. Ask yourself the following three questions:

   - *What is the worst thing that could happen if I tried this?*

   - *What is the best thing that could happen if I tried this?*

   - *What is the most realistic thing that would happen if I tried this?*

3. Visualize your new activity. In your visualization, or mental rehearsal, picture yourself doing the activity—and doing it successfully and enjoying it.

4. Schedule a time and day to undertake this new activity. Put it in your day planner or calendar.

5. If it helps, find someone to join you in your adventure.

6. Let go of all assumptions. Experience the moment as it unfolds, and don't worry about the outcome.

❧ WHEN ❧

Use this to get out of old routines and overcome what's stopping you from tapping into life's adventures, excitement, and fulfillment.

clear old emotional clutter 73

Everyone has some kind of emotional clutter—which is anything from our past that disrupts how we feel right now. This is like having a mirage appear before you, so that you react to the mirage and not to what is really in front of you. Unfortunately, emotional clutter mirages can cause emotional imbalance, confusion, and upset. To remain resilient and optimistic, you need to remove old emotional clutter, which can be as sticky as super glue.

HOW

1. Recall a past emotional clutter event that has stuck with you for years, such as how someone rejected, mistreated, or abused you.

2. Now, ask yourself these questions:

   - *How entangled am I with this clutter?*

   - *How often do I think about it each day?*

   - *In what ways does it affect how I relate to others?*

   - *How does it sap and drain my energy and focus?*

3. Take a nice, deep breath. Exhale slowly.

4. As you exhale, imagine that your out-breath is carrying the old emotional clutter, tightness, and tenseness down your legs and out of the body through the bottom of your feet. Take as many of these emotional clutter-removing breaths as you want.

5. Finally, picture a time in your life when you felt lighter, less encumbered, and more joyful—maybe you are at a favorite place or with a favorite person. Replace the old emotional clutter with the wondrous lightness of this beautiful experience. Sit with this positive feeling for a minute or longer.

WHEN

Use this when old emotional clutter keeps blocking you from the hope and optimism of this moment.

74 clear new emotional clutter

No matter how much we try to avoid new emotional clutter, it builds up daily like dust on our furniture. The only way to keep emotional clutter from accumulating is to wipe the mind clean each day. One source of ongoing emotional clutter is that which comes from technology. This is not a suggestion to avoid technology. Rather, it is an opportunity to clear away unnecessary emotional clutter.

❧ HOW ☙

1. Answer the following inventory. On average how much time *each day for the past week,* did you devote to each of the following?

   - Self-Care, including food and proper nutrition, hygiene, etc. _____

   - Communicating with significant others *face-to-face without interruption.* _____

   - On technology not for work or school, such as TV, phone, computer, laptop, etc. _____

   - Physical activity of any kind, from yoga to walking the dog. _____

   - Spending time in nature. _____

   - Hobbies, or any pleasant activity. _____

   - Reflecting, pausing, meditating, or reading. _____

   - Work or school. _____

   - Browsing and shopping, online or in a store. _____

   - Sleeping and resting. _____

2. Ask yourself:

   - *How do I feel about how I spent my time? What's most surprising?*

   - *Is technology taking time away from activities I used to enjoy, like reading or bike riding? What could bring balance?*

   - *What challenges does this present? How could I align with my deeper values?*

3. Name one small realistic change you could make starting today?

4. Notice how this change works for you and others.

❧ WHEN ❧

Use this when you wonder where your day went and didn't do anything really fun, fulfilling, or that connected you to others.

75 embrace uncertainty and rest the weary mind

Uncertainty is the keystone of life. And yet we devote hours and hours trying to control and manage a future that has not yet arrived. The truth is this: No one can purchase or own the future. This proposition is not meant to frighten, but to enlighten. The more you fear uncertainty, the more constricted, tight, and defensive you may feel. Instead, why not appreciate the uncertainty that is wrapped in each fresh, precious, and unfolding moment?

❧ HOW ❧

1. Take three soothing breaths.

2. Sit with the need for certainty about a future outcome that you have attached strongly to, but can't control. For example, this might be worrying about what your life will look like after a divorce or whether your career will continue on its present track. Ask yourself:

   How strong is my need to know?

   What would it be like for me to let it go, even for a minute?

3. For one minute, gaze up into the sky and surrender your worries about the unknown. Give it up to something infinitely wiser and larger than yourself—whether you call it God, Nature, the Mystery, or the Divine.

4. For another minute rest the weary, controlling mind. Turn your gaze toward this precious present, appreciating the gift it offers you right here and now.

5. Sit with the natural world's lessons on how there is a season for planting, growing, harvesting, and pausing. Open to these teachings in the days ahead.

❧ WHEN ❧

Embracing uncertainty is actually a life-affirming practice to use when you get wrapped up in anxiety about what is not certain anyway.

happiness

We all want happiness, but after getting our basic needs met, what we really want is the opportunity to find joy, fulfillment, and meaning, as well as to be loved, respected, and appreciated. These are the things that create happiness and buffer us against life's difficulties. When we experience happiness, we are naturally bolstered by a deep reservoir of strength, support, and resilience.

name that positive emotion 76

The mind plays an optical illusion when it comes to emotions. It focuses us more on negative emotions than positive ones. This survival tactic may have helped our ancestors remember a dangerous threat, but in today's world, joy and happiness are essential to living. Fortunately, you can rewire your brain to recall the positive—and to keep happiness at the forefront of your mind.

❧ HOW ❧

1. Get out a pad of paper, or use your smart phone. Write "Happy" at the top of the page, because this will be your Happy Emotions Journal.

2. Divide the page into three columns. Label the far left as "Positive Emotions List," label the center as "Active Emotion," and label the right column as "Event."

3. In the far left, write down all the positive emotions you can think of, such as *joy, contentment, satisfaction, happiness, bliss, awe, fun, hope, optimism, peace, calm, giddiness, amused, sympathetic, kindness, compassion, resilience, contentment, tranquility, patience, empathy, openness, acceptance,* and so on.

4. During the day, notice when you sense any of these positive emotions, writing these down in the center column. Then, in the right hand column, write in a few words what happened to elicit those feelings.

5. At the end of the week, look over your list. Notice all the positive emotions and the situations that evoked them.

6. Do this weekly until you easily recognize and feel all your positive emotions. Add more positive emotions to your list as you move forward.

❧ WHEN ❧

Use this practice to rewire your brain, increase your positive emotion vocabulary, and reboot after experiencing an especially sticky negative event.

77 wmd (weapons of mirthful delight)

The world would be a very different place, indeed, if people of all beliefs and places were intent on spreading weapons of mirthful delight, or WMD. One thing you can do is to invite WMDs into your own life, and maybe the lives of those you care about. This doesn't necessarily mean you'll laugh your way through the day (but then, who knows?). Rather, think of WMDs as load-lighteners and a way to build connections with others.

৵ HOW ৶

1. Tune in to what makes you laugh. If there is a TV program or comedian you like, arrange to see it. Schedule a laughter evening three times a week.

2. Use technology to bring WMDs to you daily. There are daily comics that you can subscribe to which come to your email inbox, comedy channels on the Internet, and various humorous videos available online.

3. Take a WMD break. Instead of mindlessly pausing, make a point of enjoying a laugh at your break time.

4. Share your WMDs. If there's a funny comic in the paper, or a funny YouTube video, consider showing it to others. Make sure, though, that it is appropriately funny and in good taste.

5. Ask about the WMDs of others. Inquire as to what tickles the funny bones of those you know. You might find a special WMD that you can enjoy from this point forward.

৵ WHEN ৶

Use WMDs to counter feeling sadness, grief, and unhappy emotions. Belly laughing WMDs can reduce pain, so use WMDs at night to lessen pain and make it easier to sleep.

b.l.e.s.s. yourself  78

If you are a parent, an adult with elderly parents, or a professional caregiver, then you know how easy it is to experience burnout and what is often known as, "compassion fatigue" or "empathy fatigue." The wear and tear of daily responsibilities can produce feelings of burnout, loss of energy, and unhappiness. The acronym B.L.E.S.S. Yourself is designed to help you recharge by turning your blessing inward.

✎ HOW ✎

1. Find a quiet place where you can spend 1-3 minutes to B.L.E.S.S. Yourself. Follow the steps below:

2. Be in the Body and Breathe. Take three long breaths to rest the busy mind and drop into the body.

3. Listen to Your Needs. Listen inwardly. Is there a wise voice of self-care or self-compassion telling you how to take care of yourself? Open up to the message that is there for you.

4. Elevate Your View. For a few moments, constructively distance, or elevate from the day-to-day caregiving mode. Imagine yourself high on a hilltop looking down at all that is happening in your life. Elevating allows you to see things in a fresh way and foster self-compassion for all you do.

5. Sense and Sensitivity. Tune into and rejuvenate yourself through all your senses. Let your senses nourish you, and be sensitive to the messages they send you telling you when they need self-care.

6. Sacred. Acknowledge the sacred in the work that you do. Breathe into the body as you feel a sense of the sacred both within and surrounding you. Sit like this for as long as you need.

✎ WHEN ✎

Use this practice when you feel burned out, emotionally depleted, and require some much needed self-soothing.

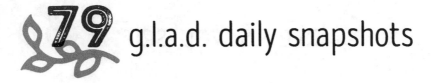

79 g.l.a.d. daily snapshots

If you want to be happy today, you have to do something about it. That's where your attention comes in to play. Attention is selective, and where you focus your attention shapes your memories and experience. It can be fun and surprising to focus on what makes you feel alive and joyful as you retrain your attention.

✎ HOW ✎

1. One Gratitude mental snapshot of:

   A basic daily life gratitude, including clothing, health, shelter, and food, etc.

   A relationship you're thankful for, such as a devoted relationship, friends, work relationships, pets, etc.

2. One snapshot of what you Learned today:

   A new insight learned about yourself or another.

   One new fact or new perspective you learned.

3. One small Accomplishment you did today:

   Self-care, such as getting enough sleep and nourishment.

   Any small step (no matter how small) toward a long-term goal.

4. One moment of Delight from today:

   Anything that makes you feel joyful or happy, such as hearing a bird chirp, seeing a flower, laughing at a joke, tasting food, returning a smile, noticing a pleasant sensation, etc.

5. Keep track of your G.L.A.D. snapshots by journaling or taking actual snapshots. Return to these weekly to bolster your memory and treasure your moments of g.l.a.d.ness.

6. Share your G.L.A.D. snapshots with friends and family, and create a family G.L.A.D. practice.

❧ WHEN ☙

Take G.L.A.D. daily snapshots in the morning to get in a positive frame of mind. Take another G.L.A.D. inventory in the evening to look back on the day. Use G.L.A.D. snapshots as daily bookends.

 morning gratitude

Mornings can be difficult for many people. If your morning starts with worry or anxious thoughts, try a morning gratitude practice. It's based on the principle that you can either choose to look at what's missing in your life, or you can choose to look at the good, basic, and beneficial things in your life—because to ignore them is to shut out life's bright and shiny side. The difficult and the beautiful co-exist, and that's okay.

৵ HOW ৵

1. Take some centering, calming breaths.

2. Notice what you are thankful for. Find something very specific that you are really, really appreciative of, including:

   • Your next precious breath.

   • The bounty of food on your table and in the refrigerator/cabinets.

   • A body that works and gets you where you want to go this morning—not to mention a car and other forms of transportation that get you where you want to go this morning.

   • Others who are in your life, who enhance this morning.

   • Find gratitude for those things you wish were not in your life and the silver linings that these provide.

3. Share your gratitude with another. Find someone who you can share your morning gratitude with, and who may be willing to share her or his morning gratitude with you.

4. Keep a journal of your morning gratitude, seeing how many different things you can be thankful for.

৵ WHEN ৵

Do this practice the first thing in the morning, in bed, or before leaving home. To have this be effective, make it a morning ritual.

sharing the (extra) ordinary with gratitude 81

Gratitude acknowledges that even the most simple, ordinary of things can possess extraordinary beauty. With gratitude, we lift the mundane into the territory of the sublime. There's research that shows paying attention to gratitude makes you happier and more optimistic. But why do this alone? Sharing gratitude with another is like plant food for the soul. It imbues your day with meaning as it helps your happiness quotient grow by leaps and bounds.

❧ HOW ❧

1. Find something ordinary that you take for granted. Be on the lookout for this throughout your day. This can be almost anything you have overlooked or become accustomed to:

   • Electricity, running water, fresh food, and even refrigeration for the food—all true gifts that are still not always available in many parts of the world.

   • Nature, from that littlest blade of grass to tallest and most majestic tree in your neighborhood.

   • Small acts of kindness, such as a smile, a kind word or gesture, and an act of generosity.

2. Pause to savor these familiar, but sensational happenings that populate the world, almost hidden from view. How marvelous!

3. Write down, take a mental snapshot, or an actual snapshot of the (extra) ordinary in your life.

4. Share your gratitude for the (extra)ordinary with a like-minded individual. Share your gratitude first, then asking your gratitude friend (at work, school, or home) what he or she appreciates. Don't be surprised if this leads to a mutual exploration about meaning and fulfillment.

❧ WHEN ❧

Share the (extra)ordinary whenever being stuck in routine leaves you feeling bored, empty, or lacking in joy.

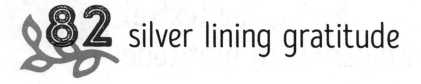# 82 silver lining gratitude

It may not be too hard to find gratitude for good things that make your life easier. But how about appreciating those things that are unpleasant, unwanted, and downright difficult? For many of us, being thankful for what you don't want in your life seems to make no sense. Silver lining gratitude, however, can brighten your life and outlook by delivering beneficial and happy surprises when and where you're least expecting them.

❧ HOW ☙

1. Find a place where you can sit in silence and with privacy.

2. Warm up by recalling a memorable and pleasant past silver lining experience that unexpectedly transformed unhappiness into joy.

3. Identify a small or major current situation causing you unhappiness. This might be anything, from an unreliable car, job, friend or partner issues, finances and retirement challenges, or any recent loss.

4. Find the silver lining. How you could be grateful for this particular instance? Suppose, for example, that you got divorced. Could you be thankful for those who made your loss more tolerable? Or, imagine if your plumbing broke. Could you be thankful for affording a plumber to repair it? Or, if you've experienced a loss, what new doors have opened for you? What possibilities are there for your personal growth?

5. How does this silver lining, or even recognizing the potential for a silver lining, make you feel?

6. Sit with your silver lining. Know that silver linings are the hope sustaining keys to finding happiness in difficult times.

❧ WHEN ☙

Turn to the silver lining gratitude practice when your happiness has been jolted by loss or difficult life challenges.

take a laughter survey

If you were an extraterrestrial being who came to Earth and discovered people engaged in laughing, what would you think was the reason for laughter? Maybe you would conduct a serious exploration to learn the purpose and benefits of laughter. To do this, you would study the places people laugh, the content of laughter, and the people who make others laugh. You might look at laughter as the most fascinating method for solving problems, boosting the immune system, and finding contentment. You might conclude that laughter is humanity's greatest discovery, one worthy of bringing back with you to the far corners of the universe. Here's how to be a laughter explorer of your own.

❧ HOW ❧

1. Keep a daily laughter journal. For an entire week, take notes on the laughter behavior that you see around you.

2. In your journal, take an inventory of all the places you find people embracing humor. With childlike curiosity, pay attention to individuals and situations, such as sporting events, shopping malls, classrooms, meetings, texts, and social media.

3. Notice the different kinds of humor. There is physical slapstick humor, wordplay, puns, sarcasm, and so on. Which of these do you find funniest? Which do you find do not really make you laugh?

4. Find a laughter resource person, or LRP. This is any individual who lightens you up and makes you smile.

5. Observe your LRP. Emulate your LRP's attitude and contact your LRP when you need a lift.

❧ WHEN ❧

Take a laughter survey to broaden your awareness of laughter and to increase the quantity of daily smiles in your life.

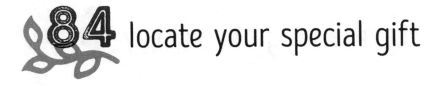

84 locate your special gift

Knowing your special personal gift is like finding a golden nugget—something precious and valuable that you possess. It could be a unique character trait, a perfectly honed skill, a specialized expertise or knowledge, or your life's purpose. Identifying your special gift is paramount to your happiness because it gives you a clearly defined sense of what you have to offer. If you haven't yet identified your gift, don't worry. It's always been there, waiting for you to claim it.

❧ HOW ☙

1. Name your gift.

   This could be a unique character trait such as the ability to listen, sing, write, dance, or feel empathy and compassion. It could be an expertise or ability, skill, hobby, or your livelihood. Be specific when naming your gift. Don't diminish your gift—even the work you do requires a skill that could be thought of as your gift.

2. Name your passion.

   This is what gets you excited and motivates you, such as working with others, being artistic or creative, building something, being innovative, and helping and caring for others. You needn't limit yourself to a single passion.

3. Express your gift once each day. If you have a gift but aren't using it fully, begin to let it shine. In this way you are being authentic and true to yourself.

4. Notice the gifts of others. Compliment others on their gifts, and remember to appreciate and compliment yourself when you express your own gift.

❧ WHEN ☙

Anytime you get that lump in your throat that makes you feel like you're not connecting with your essence, set the intention to connect with your precious gift.

share your gift 85 with purpose

Winston Churchill said, "What is the use of living, if it be not to strive for noble causes and to make this muddled world a better place for those who will live in it after we are gone?" That's why, once you've identified your gift, the next step is spreading its goodness around. Bringing your gift into the world manifests your purpose—and it is through this process that you encounter deep fulfillment and joyousness. In fact, sharing your special gift could be thought of as the very definition of purpose and attaining fulfillment and happiness.

HOW

1. Find a quiet place and get centered. Set the intention to realize your deeper purpose.

2. Reflect on your purpose. Purpose can be thought of as the integration of your gift and passion, as explored in the previous chapter. For example, if your gift is your ability style hair and your passion is to help others, then a purpose that integrates these two might be teaching others or offering to style hair for elderly or those in need.

3. Write down a one-sentence statement of your purpose that you can carry with you. There is no small or insignificant sharing of your gift.

4. Share your gift once a day for an entire week. In this way you manifest your purpose.

5. Forgive yourself in advance if you're not perfect with sharing your gift. Learning from our missteps is what makes us human, brings resilience, and gives us hope.

WHEN

Use this when you want greater fulfillment and have a desire to make a difference in the lives of others.

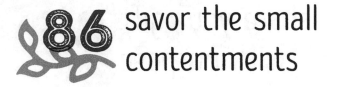# savor the small contentments

It's easy to overlook the small things in our day as unimportant filler while awaiting the "next big thing." But what if the "next big thing" was really the next small thing and the next tranquil moment? If you didn't know this, you might miss out on how there's always something big happening, even if it's small and barely noticeable. Mother Teresa referred to "the small things of daily life" as being where you find your strength. It is through relishing the small and ordinary moments of contentment that you can extinguish feelings of envy, scarcity, acquisitiveness, and other roots of unhappiness.

ஒ HOW ௸

1. Find a quiet place to sit and reflect for the next minute or two. Think of one or two small things that fit in each of the following categories:

   Small things that bring you a moment of joy. This can include the warmth of the water when showering, the smile of someone you care for, and tasting that first bite of food in the morning.

   Savor one small thing that makes you feel contented or tranquil. Happiness isn't necessarily extroverted and excitement filled, but can be felt though tranquility, including seeing the sunset, working toward a goal, enjoying a satisfying meal, and nurturing a relationship.

2. Notice a small thing or whatever brings contentment at least a couple times during the day. Write these down for later review.

3. Review these at the week's end.

ஒ WHEN ௸

Savor the small contentments throughout the day as a way to enhance your level of satisfaction and happiness with those little riches right before you.

the wishing well

Did you ever toss a few coins into a wishing well as you made a wish? There is something appealing about the idea of making a wish. The wishing well practice here doesn't even cost a penny, yet is a potent means of feeling joy for others, whether or not you agree with their life choices. This practice of wishing for the happiness of others will naturally increase your own level of happiness.

❧ HOW ☙

1. Set the intention to wish well for others who you come across this day. Each wishing well takes but seconds. This is an all-inclusive wish for all persons, regardless of their personal beliefs, political affiliation, sexual orientation, or religion.

2. Mentally recite the wishing well below. You can always adapt it, but keep it short and to the point, putting the other's happiness in the forefront of your well-wishing.

   I wish this person success and happiness on her (his) path.

   I wish this person peace and wellness.

3. Make it a point to say the blessing to anyone who angers you or upsets you today. This might, for instance, be the freeway tailgater who made an unkind gesture in your direction. What a wonderful time to practice letting go of your own judgments and biases.

4. If you are unable to say the well-wishing with an open, kind heart, take three deep breaths and try again—acknowledging that none of us is perfect and without flaws. Then, try again.

❧ WHEN ☙

Use the wishing well practice to counter negativity, pessimism, and unhappiness with others. This lets you hope for the best in all.

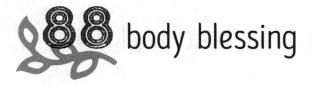 body blessing

The body is a wonderful source for finding happiness. The body's senses and functioning are quite marvelous, even if there are aspects of it that you don't like or appreciate—such as pain or how the body looks or ages. And yet, the body is your constant, devoted companion. Here's how to send a blessing to the body as you create a more sympathetic and happy relationship with it.

❧ HOW ☙

1. Find a quiet place to sit or lie down.

2. Smile inwardly at the body as you place awareness on the feet.

3. Imagine basking your feet in the warm sun or dipping them in a soothing hot springs. Let the heat soak into your feet.

4. Imagine the heat and warmth of the sun or the hot springs slowly spreading up your legs, your torso, your hands, arms and shoulders, the neck, and the head. Immerse your entire body in this warm and healing sensation.

5. Send this blessing to the body:

   I send my deepest thanks and appreciation to my body for all it does for me, and how it follows my commands without complaint so I can accomplish all I need to do each day. May I take care of this precious gift and listen for any signals it sends me, telling me that it needs attention or special care.

6. Sit for a minute or two longer, letting the body continue to feel the glow of warmth and well-being.

❧ WHEN ☙

Send a blessing to your body in the morning and end of the day, or anytime that you feel unhappy about your body.

in-joy the past

Dwelling on past negative events is a prescription for misery and dissatisfaction. Remembering positive past experiences can have the opposite effect by stimulating happy memories. To be in-joy, all you may need to do is tap your storehouse of times past. Just as ordinary and small moments can bring joy, appreciating a time when you felt proud or happy can accomplish the same thing. This is not a form of bragging, but an accurate accounting of an important personal achievement.

❧ HOW ❧

1. Find a comfortable place to sit without getting interrupted.

2. Identify a past success for which you are proud and happy. Consider any accomplishment, such as graduating from school, helping another person, displaying discipline in your job, or recovering from a setback of some kind. Even a seemingly small accomplishment is something for which you can feel proud. Consider, for example, that getting enough sleep and eating nutritiously are important and worthwhile accomplishments.

3. Spend the next one to three minutes focusing on all the details of your success. Remember what it felt like when you attained your goal or helped someone out. Let yourself feel good about your past success, noticing how this feels in your body. If you feel like smiling, go ahead.

4. Name the character qualities and strengths that enabled you to accomplish your past success. Don't be modest in noticing and naming your strengths. Think of as many as you can. Again, sit with these qualities and feel good about them.

❧ WHEN ❧

Be in-joy over a past success when you need a happiness booster shot or when you're embarking on a new goal.

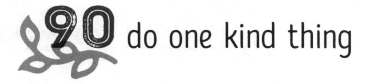 # do one kind thing

Kindness has been touched upon in several chapters of *101 Mindful Ways to Build Resilience*, and for good reason. Kindness is builder of hope and happiness. Think for a moment how the kindness of another made you feel. If it made you happy, here's your chance to pay kindness forward. This is also an opportunity to get creative because there's no one size fits all approach to being kind. Your kindness is as novel and unique as you are.

❧ HOW ☙

1. To prime your kindness pump, reflect on the following:

    Think of a recent kindness someone did for you. How did it feel? How did it make you feel about this kindness-giving person?

    Think of a recent kindness you gave to another. What did this feel like? How do you think it made the other person feel?

2. There is no small act of kindness. But if you are up for a challenge, try one of the following:

    • Compliment someone you have a problem with.

    • Anonymously buy a cup of coffee for the person waiting in line behind you.

    • When you're in a hurry, step aside and let someone get in front of you in line.

    • Talk kindly to someone you might otherwise ignore.

    • Compromise with, or forgive, someone who you disagree with.

3. Each day for a week, continue to consciously do one kind thing.

4. Keep a log of your kindnesses and share these with friends and family.

❧ WHEN ☙

Do one kind thing to see the goodness in the world, and to bring more heartfelt smiles into your life.

play your cards with skill

Sometimes, for no apparent reason whatsoever, life deals us cards that couldn't seem to be worse. Here is the secret that is often not spoken of: It isn't the cards life deals you that ultimately determine your happiness; it is your can-do attitude and interpretation of the events that transforms how you experience and play your cards. Your positive attitude, regardless of your life limitations, gives you the resilience you need.

❧ HOW ❧

1. Find a place to sit and reflect. Take three long belly breaths so you can think clearly.

2. What cards has life has dealt you? Think about these in a detached way, like a poker player might.

3. Accept the hand you are dealt. Let go of any negative feelings of blame or shame or guilt about this hand. Anger and frustration don't help you respond effectively, but could create more suffering.

4. How did you react the last time you had a similar hand? Did your reaction help or hinder you in reaching a positive outcome?

5. What can you learn from similar past life situations? Can that help you now? Even an attitude of acceptance might be all you need.

6. Assume an open attitude. Get curious about your cards. How could a shift in attitude provide you an opportunity for personal growth? What new skills and strengths could this hand of cards help you to develop?

❧ WHEN ❧

Use this anytime your options are limited or when you feel mired in negativity due to a situation in your life.

# h.e.a.r. with love

How we listen has a lot to do with our happiness in relationships. If we feel defensive toward another's viewpoint, how can we ever hope to build long-lasting bonds? The H.E.A.R. acronym (expanded in my book *Clearing Emotional Clutter*) gives you a means for hearing—and healing—with openness, empathy, love, and acceptance. If you want to build mutually satisfying relationships, it is essential to H.E.A.R. with love.

ᔶ HOW ᔷ

1. **H**old all assumptions. To begin any honest communication, you need to empty yourself of preconceived ideas and biases. It helps to just be curious about the other's perceptions and ideas.

2. **E**nter the emotional world of another with empathy. Put yourself in the other person's shoes. Let yourself feel their feelings. Empathy engages others, whereas being closed or demanding can enrage others.

3. **A**bsorb and accept. Be like a sponge that takes in all you hear. Absorbing another's perspective can take time, so absorb as much as you can. Acceptance doesn't mean you agree, but that you are open to another.

4. **R**eflect, then respect. Reflection is where you use your wisdom and insight to explore what you've heard. Sometimes it takes time to reflect, which means you may need to wait before responding. Then, bring respect, caring, and compassion into your response. If you cannot speak without anger, wait until another time when you can be respectful.

ᔶ WHEN ᔷ

Use the H.E.A.R. with love practice when you want to get beyond a damaging disagreement or misunderstanding, and you need a healthy path to reconciliation, as well as a happier and more satisfying way of relating.

pull noxious weeds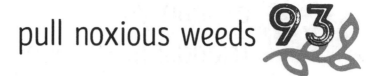

A street sign posted in the state of Oregon reads, "Pull Noxious Weeds: It's Your Responsibility." While weeds certainly need pulling, what could be more damaging than those noxious, negative, and pessimistic mental weeds that leave us feeling confused, defeated, and unhappy? This weed metaphor is a wonderful way to think about negative thinking. Weeds are normal, but rather than let them grow and choke your garden, pluck them out when they pop up. This way, they'll never get a chance to propagate in your garden of thought.

HOW

1. Label a sheet of paper with the words, "Top Ten Mental Weeds" at the top. You can always start with a "Top Three" or "Top Five" list.

2. Write down the mental weeds that grow in your mind. A weed is any thought that saps your joy or increases worry. Be on the lookout for new weeds, as well as old weeds that have been cropping up for a long time. However many mental weeds you find is fine.

3. During the day, pull the weeds. The first step here is to simply notice when you have that thought. You could even say to yourself, "Pulling the weed."

4. Put the weed into the trash. Visualize yourself putting the mental weed into a trash bin or a compactor.

5. Replace the weed with a new thought seed of your choosing. Visualize yourself planting this more helpful seed in a beautiful garden of thought.

6. Cultivate your garden daily with hopeful and positive thoughts.

WHEN

Use this whenever your garden is filled with weeds. Weed daily to keep the weeds out.

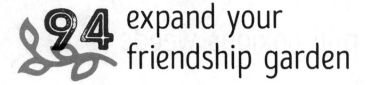 94 expand your friendship garden

In the same way that you can cultivate a beautiful garden of thought, you can expand your garden of friendships. A friendship garden can help you survive the coldest, darkest winter, when things aren't going your way. Friendships give you the sustenance necessary for ongoing resilience and happiness. Friends can transform life from what feels merely tolerable to an existence that is uplifting, enriching, and inspiring.

❧ HOW ❧

1. Assess your friendship garden. If you only have one or two friends, you might benefit from expanding the size of your garden.

2. Cast your friendship net. How will you nurture existing friends or expand your garden? Keeping in mind the activities you enjoy, consider the following ideas:
    - Church or spiritual centers
    - Book and reading clubs
    - Hiking, sightseeing, and various meet-up groups
    - Hobby clubs
    - Meditation, Yoga, and Tai Chi groups

3. Take the initiative. When you find a potential friend—or an existing one—take the initiative to ask them to meet with you.

4. Have patience. Friendships take time to develop and deepen.

5. Ask questions and take an interest. Learn about any old or new friend, and keep learning. Eventually, you can learn about an individual's history, likes, dislikes, hobbies, and more.

6. Share your life. Trust grows when you willingly share your life and experiences with your friends.

7. Laugh together. Sharing funny stories and experiences with your friends is a good way to cultivate your friendship garden.

❧ WHEN ☙

Expand your friendship garden when you are feeling isolated or need the companionship of good friends to make life more enriching and interesting.

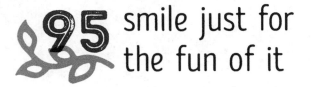# 95 smile just for the fun of it

Dr. Seuss once advised, "Don't cry because it's over. Smile because it happened." There are many good reasons to smile, and some have already been mentioned in these pages. Smiling can transform how you feel inwardly, transforming a stressful experience—like being in airports—into a pleasurable one. But you don't need a reason to smile. People may even be mystified by your change of heart and expression. Why not smile even more and just leave them guessing? When you smile, you are shining the light of happiness all around.

❧ HOW ❧

1. Practice smiling in the mirror. Who is this happy person? How does it feel when you smile?

2. Smile ear to ear. However big your smile, make an even larger one. Stretch those facial muscles and mouth until you are grinning ear to ear.

3. Don't forget to breathe. Belly breathe three times as you smile. Feel the nice release as you exhale, keeping your smile during the entire breath.

4. Practice real-world smiling. Smile in the morning when you awaken. Smile as you walk down the street. Whether or not others respond is not the point. Remember, you are smiling for the fun of it.

5. Smile at people from your car. Even though other drivers may not see you, smile anyway. Can you really get upset at the traffic congestion when you're smiling?

6. Smile at the difficulties. Smile at your computer when it crashes. Smile at the person who doesn't like you.

7. Don't forget to smile at those who like, admire, and love you!

❧ WHEN ❧

Anytime, for the fun of it.

tap nature's splendor

Did you ever wonder why you feel better after spending some time in nature? Research shows that nature calms and soothes. It restores your brain's ability to focus and concentrate. Perhaps the most important reason for tapping into nature is that it is an enduring touchstone that connects us to the nurturing source of all life and this living planet that sustains us. As long as we are children of an Earth mother, there can be no substitute for nature's touch.

ଡ଼ HOW ଡ଼

1. Sit or stand in a natural setting. This can be the small garden in a business park, the grassy patch along the sidewalk, or your own backyard.

2. Begin by casting your gaze up into the sky or horizon. Do this with a sense of wonderment at the vastness of the sky.

3. Let go your worries. Surrender them to nature's spaciousness, which is infinitely large and able to hold these while you rest your weary mind.

4. Move your gaze to a tree or plant. Starting from the plant's top, move your gaze slowly downward. Notice the uniqueness of the leaves, branches, and bark.

5. Touch this plant or tree. Let yourself feel the peace and steadiness of it. Notice how rooted and stable it is.

6. Let the steadiness seep and absorb into your body. Feel your feet solidly rooted to the ground. Let this pleasant feeling of peace, connectedness, and grounding permeate your whole being.

ଡ଼ WHEN ଡ଼

Tap nature's joy in the morning, midday, and evening—especially when you've been indoors, are feeling disconnected, or can't focus and think clearly.

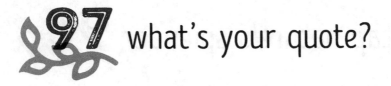# 97 what's your quote?

Do you have a favorite or special quote that inspires and motivates you? How about a favorite quote that enhances hopefulness and optimism? How about one that invites a sense of peace and contentment? Humanity's collective wisdom and humor stretches back centuries. Thanks to technology, finding that perfect quote may just be a few computer clicks away. Even if you already have a favorite quote, here's how to use your quotes to bolster happiness and a wise perspective—almost instantly.

HOW

1. Find your quotes. What quotes sound like something you could have written? Is there someone you admire whose sentiments and values align with yours? Whether your quotes are wise, irreverent, profound, insightful, clever, glib, silly, confounding, or thought provoking, make sure they feel in harmony with your mind and body.

2. Post your quote where you (or others) can see it. Add a quote to your computer signature, as a note taped on your wall, or as reminder to carry in your purse or wallet.

3. Express your quotes. Think about how you can live the essence of your favorite quotes each day—even in a small way.

4. Share your favorite quotes. Give others who know you copies of your favorite quotes, and find out what quotations others like most. You can learn a lot about someone by the quotations they keep.

5. Expand your favorite quotes. Embrace a new quote for a week at a time and see how each quote manifests in your thinking and actions.

WHEN

Use this "what's your quote" practice to stay inspired, joyful, and express your authentic self.

see the precious 98
one at your side

One of the world's greatest magic tricks is performed before us each day. The illusion is this: That tomorrow will be much like today. It's a great illusion because certain constants seem to repeat forever, like the sun always rising and falling in the sky. Soon, we begin to think that other important things will last forever, like the people in our lives. The real trick is realizing that the only time that matters is now—which makes the one at your side that much more special and precious.

❧ HOW ❧

1. Take the microscopic inner view. If you could peer deeply inside another's brain, you would find it contains more than 100 billion neurons, and more connections among these neurons than there are stars in the known universe. That means the person beside you is the most unique and precious individual in the universe—as are you.

2. Say hello with love and kind regards. Let this precious one know how you feel.

3. Treat this precious one with care, kindness, and respect. Let each interaction with another express the best of who you are.

4. Help this precious one. What one helpful thing could you do for this person? Helping brings meaning and happiness to others as well as yourself.

5. Say goodbye with love. Don't take this precious one for granted. Bid goodbye with a smile, touch, hug, or caring words.

❧ WHEN ❧

This is a good practice to use whenever you meet another person, or want to shift your experience of this moment into the realm of the sublime.

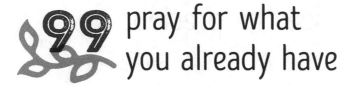# 99 pray for what you already have

We've all rejected things in our lives at one point or another. Maybe you rejected someone who wanted to date you. Maybe you rejected the meal on your plate when you saw the more appetizing one your friend ordered. Or maybe you pushed away a meditation because it was too noisy. One way to enhance joy is to pray for what you already have in your life. This is living without resistance, without fighting against the moment. It's easier than you think, and it gives you an entirely fresh view.

HOW

1. Find a place to sit and reflect in quiet.

2. Identify what you're rejecting. For example, maybe you're not in the house of your dreams or the career of your dreams.

3. Accept what is in your life. Let in the blessings that are present. Your home may not be ideal, but you have shelter, which is more than what some possess.

4. Appreciate what you do have. Your career or job may be flawed, but it is a starting point, and might be more than what others enjoy.

5. Embrace the ups and downs as temporary. Look around and find others who face challenges much greater than your own. This can help you recognize what your life would be like if the things you reject were taken away.

6. Notice all the imperfect, yet useful things that exist for you. Look around and find how recognizing these blessings brightens your day.

WHEN

Pray for what you already when you want to overcome self-criticism or complaints that diminish your happiness.

start anew

No one succeeds one hundred percent of the time. A baseball player who gets a hit one out of every three times gets in baseball's Hall of Fame. That means they fail two-thirds of the time. Basketball superstar Michael Jordan missed far more shots than he made. What gives superstars the confidence and the resilience to be the best—when they fail more often than not? The secret it simple: They are excellent at forgetting that last mistake and starting anew. By starting anew they remain happier, confident, and positive.

❧ HOW ☙

1. Prepare the best you can. Solid preparation doesn't mean you will always hit your mark, but it does mean you can trust your skills and feel confident enough to start anew and be effective over time.

2. Practice, practice, practice. If you want to start anew, it helps to put in practice. With enough practice, you can trust on your mind and body to learn the lessons that are needed when you start anew.

3. Be kind and forgive yourself. A perfectionist attitude creates anxiety and feelings of blame. A more forgiving attitude helps you be at ease and perform better.

4. Let go of the outcome. Any mistake only means you can make corrections and get back on the right path. Starting anew is simply a course correction on the journey.

5. Embrace the journey with joy. Starting anew lets you get more present. It lets you leave the past behind and try again with hope and joy.

❧ WHEN ☙

Start anew whenever you need the confidence to get past self-doubt and anxiety—and locate joy.

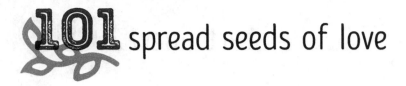 **spread seeds of love**

Right now, take a few moments to stroll down memory lane. Who is especially dear to you? What did these folks do to produce warm-hearted and enduring feelings, even years afterwards? Likely, they knew how to spread seeds of love. The Buddha said, "Hatred does not cease by hatred, but only by love; this is the eternal rule." It's easy to underestimate love. Love is the elixir that touches the heart, warms the body, and stirs hope in all of us—that one day the world may find peace and happiness.

❧ HOW ❧

1. Love, naturally, starts at home. Say the following two lines to yourself over and over until you feel the meaning seeping into you. Feel the warm glow of this blessing in your body.

   May I be understood and accepted.

   May I be nurtured and loved.

   If you have a hard time feeling this, picture yourself as a baby or child who deserved love. Then, say these words for that baby or child.

2. Say the following words over and over for others for a short time.

   May all beings be understood and accepted.

   May all beings be nurtured and loved.

3. Write a note to one you care about. Write a handwritten note expressing thanks or gratitude for something this person has done for you—or for how they have shown you love.

4. Repeat this blessing for yourself each day, and also for others.

5. Each day, take the time to express love toward someone.

❧ WHEN ❧

Practice this sentiment throughout the day, or to help you see that we are all deserving of love.